Crushing It with Social Media Marketing and Personal Branding

Discover Top Entrepreneur and Influencer Viral Network and SEO Secrets for YouTube, Instagram, and Facebook Advertising (Ads)

Gary Donald

Legal Notice:

This book is copyright protected. This book is only for personal use. You cannot amend, distribute, sell, use, quote or paraphrase any part, or the content within this book, without the consent of the author or publisher.

Disclaimer Notice:

Please note the information contained within this document is for educational and entertainment purposes only. All effort has been executed to present accurate, up to date, and reliable, complete information. No warranties of any kind are declared or implied. Readers acknowledge that the author is not engaging in the rendering of legal, financial, medical or professional advice. The content within this book has been derived from various sources. Please consult a licensed professional before attempting any techniques outlined in this book.

By reading this document, the reader agrees that under no circumstances is the author responsible for any losses, direct or indirect, which are incurred as a result of the use of information contained within this document, including, but not limited to, — errors, omissions, or inaccuracies.

Contents

2 IN 1 VALUE

CRUSHING IT
WITH SOCIAL MEDIA MARKETING
AND
PERSONAL BRANDING

TARGET

ONLINE MARKETING

CUSTOMER

DISCOVER TOP
ENTREPRENEUR AND INFLUENCER
VIRAL NETWORK AND SEO SECRETS
FOR YOUTUBE, INSTAGRAM, AND
FACEBOOK ADVERTISING (ADS)

SALES

PLAN

CREATIVITY

COMMUNICATION

MARKETING

GARY DONALD

Crushing It with Social Media Marketing

Discover Top Entrepreneur Viral Network and SEO Strategies for YouTube, Instagram, Facebook, Twitter While Advertising Your Personal Brand and Business

Gary Donald

Chapter 1:
Social Media Marketing Explained in 15 Minutes

Social Media Marketing is a kind of internet marketing that exploits social networking websites as a tool for the promotion of sites. This, in turn, enhances traffic towards them, allowing them to learn from the direct reaction of users.

In recent years, social media has become an essential agent in the growth of businesses worldwide. Yes, social media marketing is gradually becoming a trend among organizations.

Social media marketing, simply defined, has to do with promotional activities which take place through social media channels, like blogs, social media networks and online discussion groups.

Social Media Marketing has to do with the principle of organic search. It means that when a site or its linked social network page has more activity, the position of the website on search engines goes up in their search results, perhaps even making it to the first page.

Seeing as more than 80 percent of users searching the web don't search any further than the first page of search results, and that 70 percent click only on the first three choices, it is apparent that aiming to get on the first page of search results should be your primary goal when optimizing a site.

What Is SMM Used For?

The major objective of Social Media Marketing is to enhance interaction with users, boost the visibility of brands and reach more potential clients.

Social Media Marketing is done by developing quality content which social network users will be able to share with their friends through the transmission of information electronically.

The essence of social media marketing it to obtain feedback from users or possible clients directly so that the company appears more human-like.

By using interactive options on social networks, clients can be heard, either by making complaints or asking questions. This kind of social media marketing is known as Social CRM (customer relationship management) and can result in boosting ROI and credibility. Of course, this is only applicable if users are satisfied with the relationship with the organization, content and the service offered.

Social Networking Sites

Gary Donald

Social networking sites allow businesses, individuals and other organizations to communicate with each other and grow communities and relationships online. When organizations become a part of these social platforms, customers will be able to interact with them directly. This level of interaction tends to be more personal to users as opposed to the standard method of advertising and inbound marketing.

The ability of the internet to reach almost anyone across the world has offered the online word of mouth an extensive reach and a powerful voice. The ability to quickly change service or product acquisition, buying patterns and activity to a growing number of customers is said to be an influence network.

Social networking websites and blogs give followers the ability to repost and retweet comments others make in regards a product being promoted, which takes place a lot on social media websites. By posting publicly, friends of these users will also be able to view the message, thus getting across to more individuals. Because product information is being exposed and repeated, it leads to more traffic for the company or product.

Social networking sites are based on developing virtual environments which let customers express their values, wants and needs online. Social media marketing then links these audiences and consumers to organizations that have similar wants, needs, and values.

Using social networking websites, companies can stay in touch with followers individually. This level of personal interaction can inspire a sense of loyalty in followers and possible clients. Additionally, by deciding who to follow on these websites, products can reach a very more targeted audience.

Social networking websites also consist of lots of information regarding what services and products prospective customers may have an interest in. Using new semantic analysis technologies, marketers will have the ability to point out buying signals from questions posted online and content shared by individuals.

A knowledge of how buying signals work can aid sales individuals in targeting prospective clients. In can also aid marketers in running micro-targeted campaigns.

In 2014, more than 70 percent of the business executives singled out social media as a core aspect of their organizations. What is more, business retailers have observed over 100 percent increases in their earnings from social media marketing.

What Are the Most Recognized Platforms of Social Media?

The most popular websites for social networking that businesses can benefit from include:

- Facebook – which has more than 2 billion users

- YouTube – the biggest site for video networking with more than a billion active users monthly

- Instagram – sharing of images with more than 800 million users monthly

- Twitter – broadcasting of messages with more than 300 million active users

- WhatsApp – audio, messaging and video communications with more than one billion users

- LinkedIn – the biggest network of business professionals with more than 400 million members

- Pinterest – Image sharing and collection with more than 150 million active users monthly

- Quora – knowledge and information exchange

- Tumblr – photo sharing and blogging

Benefits of Social Media Marketing to Your Business

Nowadays, almost every individual is on one form of social media or another, irrespective of if this is Twitter, Instagram or Facebook. Social media has become a modern wonder, and instead of being utilized solely for communication which it once was, social media has become a core aspect of any individual who is getting into the world of business.

Now, organizations know how to utilize social media and promote themselves in the best way possible to their potential audience. If you know how to exploit social media, it can become a fantastic tool that will aid in growing your brand.

But, if you still don't see any reason why your business needs a social media page, let us look at some of the reasons why.

Enhanced Brand Awareness

Social media is one of the budget-friendliest methods of digital marketing utilized in syndicating content and enhancing the visibility of your brand. Executing a strategy on social media will significantly improve the recognition of your brand because you will be engaging with a broad consumer audience.

To begin, develop social media profiles for your organization and start to interact with others. Get business partners, employees as well as sponsors to share and like your page. Just by having individuals interact with your content, your brand awareness will go up and start to grow your business reputation.

A new network of individuals is likely to see each shared post. This can result in them becoming potential clients. What is more, the more individuals who know about your organization and what you do, the better. By investing just a few hours weekly, more than 90 percent of marketers claim that their efforts on social marketing tremendously enhanced their exposure.

Without a doubt, just having a social media page for your brand will be beneficial to your business. Also, with frequent use, it can produce a broad audience for your business.

Increase in Inbound Traffic

If you do not market your organization on social media, your inbound traffic will be restricted to your regular clients. The individuals who know your brand are possibly looking for similar keywords you rank for already. If you do not use social media as an aspect of your marketing strategy, you will find it more difficult to reach individuals who are not in the circle of your loyal customers.

Each social media profile you include to your marketing mix opens a path to your website, and each content piece you post is another chance of getting a new client. Social media is a place filled with various kinds of individuals who come from diverse backgrounds with varying behaviors.

With different individuals come varying needs and diverse methods of thinking. Placing your content on as many platforms as you can lets these individuals reach your business organically. Perhaps a person in an older consumer demographic will look for your site using a specific keyword on Facebook, but a younger client may start their search by utilizing another platform of social media entirely because they don't search for products the same way.

When you market on social media, you can open your business to a broader range of varying customers around the globe.

Enhanced Rankings on Search Engines

When you post on social media, it may help your business gain some traffic. But if you want a significant level of success, you would have to put in more effort than that. Search engine optimization is crucial for attaining higher rankings on your page and drawing traffic to the site of your business.

Although social media does not increase search engine rankings directly, it was stated by Social Media Examiner that over 50 percent of marketers who have been utilizing social media for a year or more would see better search engine rankings. The ability to rank lead positions for keywords will transform your traffic and keep producing positive results for your organization.

Speaking factually, almost everyone utilizes Google in finding information, and there is less likelihood of them navigating further than the first page because they usually find the solution to their queries there.

If the website of your organization does not have a high ranking on search engine results, you may likely have to make changes to your SEO strategy, so that you have the best possibility of getting a better ranking via social media. To do this, you need to produce content of high-quality that incorporates your target keywords.

Content like case studies, infographics, employee photos, and business information will make the social media profile of your business credible and exciting. The instant you start posting content of high-quality, you will begin to grow a social media environment where followers will share and like your content.

The important part is, it gives you the chance to get in front of industry influencers who will write about your organization and offer linkbacks which will aid directly in enhancing rankings on search engines.

Higher Rate of Conversion

When your business has more visibility, it will have more chances for conversion. Every video, image, comment or blog post may direct viewers to the website of your organization and enhance traffic. Social media marketing lets your business offer a positive impression by utilizing a humanization factor.

When a brand is interactive by commenting, sharing content and posting statuses on social media, it helps personalize it. Individuals would instead do business with other individuals as opposed to companies. Over 50 percent of marketers made claims that taking the effort to groom relationships with customers proved positive results in sales.

The better your impression on a visitor, the higher the probability of them thinking about your organization when the need for your services or products arises. According to studies, social media has a 100 percent higher lead-close rate as opposed to outbound marketing. When a brand has more interaction online, customers who follow the accounts of your brand often start to trust your business's credibility more. People generally utilize social media platforms to remain connected to their family, friends, and communities. Since individuals are interacting already, why not add your brand to the conversation? Most times, they will tell a friend about your brand when your services and products are required.

Placing your brand in an environment where individuals are talking, liking and sharing can only enhance the rate of conversion on your present traffic.

Enhanced Customer Satisfaction

Social media is a platform for communication and networking. It is crucial to create a voice for your company via this platform if you want to humanize your organization.

Customers love knowing that any comments they post on your page will get a personalized response as opposed to an automated message. The ability to acknowledge every comment show that you listen to the needs of your visitors and have the goal of providing them with a peak experience.

Each customer interaction on the social media account of your organization is a chance to publicly show how compassionate you are to your customers. Whether a person has a complaint or question, social media lets you deal with the matter utilizing interpersonal conversation. A brand dedicated to the satisfaction of customers, which takes time to write a personal message, will be seen in a positive light, even if responding to the complaints of a customer.

Enhanced Brand Loyalty

One of the core objectives of almost all organizations is creating a loyal customer base. Considering that brand loyalty and customer satisfaction go alongside one another, it is crucial to engage customers regularly and start creating a bond with them.

Social media is not just restricted to introducing the promotional campaigns and products of your brand. Customers view these platforms as a channel where they will be able to communicate with the business directly.

The millennial generation has the most brand loyal customers. They make up a more substantial portion of the US and will soon take over the market entirely. According to studies, this group of customers is more than 60 percent loyal to brands that interact with them directly on social media.

Since this group needs communication with their brands, it is essential that organizations implement social media marketing to draw their attention as they are the consumers with the most influence.

Increased Brand Authority

Brand loyalty and customer satisfaction have a role to play in ensuring your business is more authoritative, but it all boils down to communication. When consumers observe that your organization posts on social media, especially posting authentic content and replying to customers, it makes you seem more credible.

Frequently communicating with customers shows that your organization cares about the satisfaction of clients and is available to provide answers to any queries they may have. Happy customers are elated to spread the word about a fantastic service or product, and social media is the location they usually head to to express their thoughts.

When customers mention your organization on social media, it will aid in advertising your organization and show new visitors your brand's authority and value. As soon as you can get some satisfied clients who are happy to talk about their excellent buying experience, you can sit back and watch real customers who benefited from your service or product do the advertising.

Cost-Efficient

Social media marketing is perhaps the most cost-effective aspect of an advertising strategy. It is free to sign up and create a profile for almost all platforms for social networking. Also, any paid promotion you decide to invest in does not cost that much in comparison to other marketing strategies.

Being cost-efficient is such a great benefit because you experience more ROI and invest a larger budget for other business and marketing expenses. If you choose to go with paid advertising on social media, it is crucial you begin small to see what is to be expected. As you become relaxed, make changes to your strategy and try adding more to the budget. By spending a little amount of money and time, you can drastically enhance your rates of conversion and get a return on your initial investment.

Attain Insights to The Marketplace

One of the most significant benefits of social media is marketplace insight. There are no better methods of knowing what your customers need and think than by speaking to them directly. By observing your profile's activities, you will be able to see the opinions and interests of customers that you would not have previously been aware of if your business had no presence on social media.

Using social media as a support tool for research can aid in gaining valuable data that will help you better understand the industry, once you have amassed a considerable following, you will be able to use additional tools to investigate your consumers demographic.

Another aspect of social media marketing, which is quite insightful, is the ability to section your content syndication lists based on topic and point out the kinds of content that amass the most impressions. With these tools, you will have the ability to measure conversions using posts on a variety of social media platforms to find the ideal mix to increase earnings.

Thought Leadership

Posting properly written and insightful content on your social media page is a fantastic method of becoming a leader and expert in your industry. Becoming a leader requires work, and you can get assistance by using online tools. To become an expert, you need to make use of social media channels and develop your presence.

Be interactive, share content, bond with your audience and promote your authority. When your social media campaign aligns with your other marketing efforts, it will highlight your skills and your audience will look up to you. The ability to connect with your customers directly results in a relationship that they will find valuable. This lets you become a recognized influencer in your sector.

Chapter 2:
Double Down on Social Media Marketing NOW

Lots of businesses are cautious about the kind of marketing strategies they spend on. When your marketing budget is limited, it is crucial that you wisely spend it to get the best from your investment. Social media marketing is one of the most cost-effective and versatile strategies that businesses can utilize in reaching their target audience and enhance sales over time. This is the reason more than 90 percent of marketers are utilizing social media to get to their audiences.

So why do businesses need to double down on social media now? Below are a few reasons why it is compulsory for small businesses.

You Will Find Your Customers on Social Media
One of the primary reasons why your business must be marketed via social media is because your clients spend lots of time on these platforms. The number of individuals using social media is on the rise, and with lots of customers utilizing social media daily, this offers an excellent chance for businesses who want to reach their audience online.

It can be easy to connect with your target audience if you are active on the platforms that they utilize most frequently. Go to your audience as opposed to waiting for them to come to you. If you are not on social media already, you are probably missing out on a crucial opportunity to interact with new leads and connect with your clients.

Clients Are More Receptive on Social Media

Individuals who are active on social media channels do so because these platforms provide an easy and entertaining method of networking, keeping in touch with family and friends, and keeping abreast of things going on around the globe. Users don't join these channels to get marketed to, but it does not imply that users of social media don't follow and interact with the brands they love.

When users engage and follow brands, it is because they see the information and content in these social media campaigns relevant. Whether these users are enjoying entertaining content, in search of deals or just want to find out more regarding the brands, social media users are more likely to engage with brands through their social media channels.

Clients tend to be more receptive to the message of your brand on social media because social media lets you show another aspect of it. The content you release on these channels contributes to the personality of your brand and aids in demonstrating your brand's voice.

Via social media, you will have the ability to make a real connection with your customers and leads, as opposed to just sending direct marketing messages. Clients are more responsive to this sort of thing.

Advertising on Social Media Lets You Target and Retarget Perfect Customers

Although social media marketing does not need any investment in advance, social ads can do much to support your existing organic campaigns on your social media channels. Using refined targeting capabilities, social media channels like Facebook aids you in targeting your perfect buyers, which lets you push more significant traffic to your website. This is the ideal method of getting the best from your marketing investment.

Through Facebook ads, you can point out new possible leads by defining your perfect customers using the ads platform. Also, Facebook lets you serve your ad content to individuals who show the same kinds of attitude your target audience does. As you push more significant traffic to the website of your brand, you will be able to enhance the results, irrespective of what your ad objectives are.

You Will Find Your Competition on Social Media

Irrespective of the sector you are in or your target market, there is a huge possibility that your competitors are there already and taking advantage of social media platforms. This not only shows that there is a chance for your brand to equally perform well on these platforms, but it also implies that some of your potential clients may be speaking to the competition already.

If you need to stay competitive in the online marketplace, it is crucial that you begin working towards the establishment of a social media presence. Social media content not only gives you the chance to show a little part of your brand's personality, but it also offers an excellent channel for showing your industry knowledge and expertise. This is one of the best methods of making yourself stand out from the competition and bringing in more significant online traffic.

Social Media Marketing Results in Higher Rates of Conversion

Social media has a 100 percent higher close rate than outbound marketing strategies. This could be because every piece of content you upload and interaction you may have on your social media platforms is a chance to transform an attracted lead into a satisfied customer.

By developing rapport with your customers and leads, and posting relevant content consistently, your brand will be able to work at improving credibility and trust, which results in more conversions.

The most important aspect of social media that leads to more conversions is the ability to add a more human element to your brand's messaging. Because social media is a location for customers to network and socialize, brands can show their human side through conversation and simple content that shows their warmth, humor, and personality.

Gary Donald

Customers Are in Search of Recommendations on Social Media

WOM (word of mouth) marketing is one of the most reliable tools that any organization has in its marketing arsenal. Aside from the fact that it is free, it goes further in aiding you to develop credibility with new leads. In lots of ways, social media has transformed into a new environment for word-of-mouth marketing. Now, brands are starting to encourage their clients to leave reviews on their social media pages, offer testimonials or recommend their brand to family and friends on social media.

Consumers have a higher possibility of purchasing from brands that others recommend. These recommendations don't have to be from a family member, friend, or co-worker. Consumers have as much a likelihood of trusting online reviews as they would personal recommendations.

Customers are always searching for recommendations on social media, and these recommendations affect their buying behavior. This is why it is crucial that you continue encouraging your satisfied customers to leave a review for your brand on social media and recommend your services and products to others. This is a fantastic method of generating some of that significant word of mouth benefit that aids in increasing sales.

Social Media Can Help Link Your Brand to Clients You Never Knew Existed

Lots of brands depend on PPC ad traffic and search engine optimization to locate and engage new leads. But, marketing via social media can be a fantastic channel for drawing in new clients. Reviews or recommendations on social media can go far in aiding your brand link with customers whom you never knew existed.

Your company can also utilize social media to tap into new markets through other ways. One method of locating new market opportunities and customers on your social platforms is via social listening. By following specific keywords and searching trending subjects in your sector, you will be able to see who is partaking in the conversation. This can aid in providing your organization with loads of chances for new leads while equally connecting you to influencers in the industry which you may be able to collaborate with to enhance visibility.

Top Social Media Marketing Strategies

The factors that constitute efficient social media marketing differ. They depend on a range of factors which include current trends, and your goals alongside your audience. These factors define what your plan of action or strategy to achieve a specific goal should be.

Below are a few of the tried and tested strategies that are almost certain to work alongside other upcoming strategies that can help you keep up with the changing trends.

Developing Different Kinds of Content

It is quite easy to get sucked into only posting brief tweets on Twitter or pictures on Facebook. However, on most social media channels, you can post diverse kinds of content which include infographics, blog posts, and videos. So why do you need to do this?

For one, creating the same form of content without end can bore your audience which will prevent you from attaining your goals. You are going to get the same results you have already if you create the kind of content that echoes with just a part of your audience or worse still, none.

By ensuring your posts vary, you will be able to determine the top kinds of content for your target audience and easily appeal to all its subsets.

Offer Education
Irrespective of the goals you have, offering education is almost the best means of helping you attain them. If you provide relevant information or great advice, individuals will see you as an authority and will likely become loyal clients with time.

You can educate your followers on social media itself or by utilizing your accounts to lead engaged followers to educational resources like webinars, online courses, white papers among others.

Do Less Promotion and More Storytelling?
Going the educational route implies that you will be teaching more as opposed to selling. Storytelling is along the same lines and can be

educational. But the strength of storytelling is not in teaching individuals' things they were not aware of but informing them about situations or characters that they can relate with and draw out emotional responses. These kinds of reactions trigger action, usually more effective than continuous and annoying self-promotion on social media.

Use Influencer Marketing

Collaborating with well-connected and renowned influencers is an excellent choice for numerous reasons. Two major advantages are:

It enhances your credibility and provides you access to a broader audience, both of which can aid in making your strategy for social media marketing more efficient.

Take Advantage of The Eagerness of Loyal Clients

Your loyal customers have lots of power. They also can become advocates for your brand. They can enhance your brand awareness and offer great social proof, aiding other customers in developing trust in your organization faster than they would have initially.

Social media is a great tool when used by motivated brand advocates. However, you must be the one to motivate them. You can do this by:

- Requesting reviews on social networks like Instagram and Facebook

- Ensuring the submission of great content generated by users, which can then be utilized in your social media campaigns

- Granting interviews to satisfied clients and publishing their stories to your pages on social media

- Setting up contests and providing rewards, which would then inspire individuals to spread the word regarding your organization on the social media platforms you decide.

These are just a few of the choices you must take advantage of.

Best Upcoming Social Media Marketing Strategies
Yes, lots of strategies that have worked in the past can still work now. However, you need to understand that as technology and trends go through change, you need to implement new strategies. So, what are the strategies for social media marketing you need to take advantage of? Below are a few of them:

Augmented and Virtual Reality
The interest consumers are starting to have in immersive experiences is beginning to rise. Due to this, both AR, augmented reality, and VR, virtual reality, are beginning to be used more as tools for marketing. This could either be via absolute immersion experiences that take you to a world of your own (VR) or via digital factors including a live view (AR). Numerous brands are enhancing audience engagement in this way.

Taking advantage of mobile cameras in this method can give your potential clients the chance to experience and understand your services and products in the same way they would in real life. You would be able to have a direct influence on their purchasing choices, which would have obvious advantages to your organization.

If you have not done so yet, you need to think of ways to include VR/AR into your strategy for social media to achieve your goals in the coming years.

Live Streaming

Live streaming has existed for some time now, but it is still something that needs more emphasis. This is because more than 70 percent of brand audiences would rather choose live video instead of social posts and blog posts.

Generally, as videos keep rising in popularity, you can be confident that there will only be an increase in this presence. Now is the best time to place more focus on streaming and learn to master it

Social TV & Vertical Videos

Lots of social channels are now focusing on vertical videos because people use their phones vertically most of the times. This recent focus goes alongside something else that is gaining popularity known as social TV.

Leading this trend presently is Instagram with the newly released IGTV. It lets users develop channels and upload long videos there. Snap originals and YouTube TV are also similar kinds of social TV, although not presently available to the multitudes.

Still, long-form and vertical videos are things you should consider creating, especially if you promote your business using Instagram and want to try out IGTV.

Enhanced Humanization

Individuals tend to have a strong response to others. If you humanize your brand on social media, you will be able to create a more effective marketing strategy. How do you do this? Well, you need to communicate with your followers as much as you can by using content generated by users, responding to comments, etc. Although these things have already been recommended, it is now more critical than ever.

Chatbots

Chatbots will undoubtedly become more popular on social media in the future. You can use these bots to respond to questions, urge unlikely sales, begin conversations and offer individualized customer support and service.

By incorporating this social media strategy when only a few individuals are utilizing it, you can drastically enhance your results and appeal on social media.

Stories Will Grow More Popular

Stories are now on the rise. Viewing visual content in a vertical layout which lasts for just 24 hours started making waves on Snapchat and soon Instagram followed suit which made it a world trend for individuals of all ages.

Snapchat may have battled since then to stay relevant since that is what it is known for, but now, stories are now on Facebook, Instagram, YouTube and LinkedIn.

Presently, there are over 300 million individuals benefiting from Instagram stories daily, while Facebook is making efforts to incorporate stories in our daily life.

Advertisers have also observed that Instagram Stories ads can be quite efficient, with Facebook and Snapchat keeping up with their present demand hype. So why are stories so great?

- They are not difficult to make

- They depend on authenticity

- They are entertaining

- They don't need more editing before you upload

- They don't last past 24 hours

Messaging Will Rise Even More

In usage, messaging apps have already surpassed social media applications in terms of usage, and it looks like a trend that will dominate the future. People are going past social media posts to private messaging. This is the case simply if it has to do with reaching their loved ones or keeping up with their best celebrities.

What makes messaging appealing is the fact that brands can locate the engagement they desire by understanding how individuals utilize messaging applications.

Earlier in 2017, marketers were of the belief that messaging is the pioneer trend that will have an impact on their social strategies. Messaging, Viber, WhatsApp and WeChat have a huge part of the messaging market and they already unleashed extra features to go past messaging, from news updates and stories to utilizing automated bots for e-commerce and customer service roles.

There is an entire world for brands to take advantage of and lots of huge publishers and brands are starting to exploit the messaging trend.

Chapter 3:
How to Start Social Media Marketing with No Experience

While making attempts at growing your business, you have concluded that having a strong presence on social media is how to make this happen. Now, a question arises. How do you set about it?

Making your first move on a social media platform is not the easiest of things. There are lots of platforms, as well as sites. These are in addition to the huge number of social media users, and an overwhelming amount of content to check out.

With this, how exactly do you get started? Do you have an exact reason for promoting your business?

It is quite a lot to think about. Below are tips to help beginners with social media marketing.

Set Out with A Primary Objective

There are some critical questions that you must provide answers to if you want to take advantage of social media. What do you plan to achieve? Do you plan to up customer service, or make better sales?

Are you also considering the option of getting your brand into the minds of people?

If you can provide answers to these questions, then, your efforts on social media will be in a guided direction. As the months and years go by, you will have to put more time into social media. As a result of this, you should start with your fundamental objective. This will help you measure the progress you make.

Take One Step At A Time And Be Choosy
There are a lot of social media platforms. Popular among them are LinkedIn, Facebook, Instagram, Twitter, etc. If you have big dreams, there is a likelihood you will want to take advantage of the most famous social media platforms. Well, the truth remains it will be impossible to do so. Don't try to have a presence on all social media platforms all at once. You must take things slowly.

Be careful how you choose. Start with a couple of sites first. These should be the most ideal for the kind of business you do. As soon as you can put in more time, as well as money, get on other platforms and make your business known.

It Is Not Enough to Be on A Platform
It is vital that you have an audience in mind. As you come up with strategies, the question "Who is your audience?" will be a great guide.

This question will influence how you strategize. Think about your choice of site for a second. If your target audience are millennials, platforms such as Instagram, Snapchat, and YouTube will be ideal. Pinterest is surprisingly good if moms are your target. With Facebook, you can reach virtually everyone.

What social platform will be ideal? Well, the answer to this question is dependent on the business you at running. Carry out intensive research on your target audience before making important decisions such as where to put your efforts.

You Should Have A Catchy Handle

If a handle is memorable and catchy, it will stick in the minds of people. As far as your presence on social media is concerned, you should have a handle that can be easily attributed to your brand irrespective of what platform it is on.

You could decide to make use of the name of your company. You could also use something that brings attention to the unique quality that your brand possesses. An example of this is that the BBC makes use of @BBCBreaking as its account name on Twitter. This brings breaking news to the minds of people. Also, Samsung makes use of @Samsung-Mobile. This reminds consumers about the existence of their mobile devices.

What Is the Ideal Handle for Your Business?

As soon as you have decided on the handle to use, carry out adequate research to make sure that it has not been taken on the social media platforms you are getting on. You can get this done using Knowem.

Get A Social Media Team
When you come up with a plan for going into social media marketing, you must create a social media team. You will also need funds to make this a reality. After your presence on social media becomes prominent, handling it all by yourself will be very difficult. You will need to work with people and focus on the actual running of your business.

Make attempts at building a team of professionals with very different qualities. This team should have a writer that can create social content which is compelling, and a video and graphics group that can handle multimedia. That is not all. An expert at analytics will also be needed on your team. This expert will take note of your progress, as well as the weaknesses he sees in your social media campaign. A lot of small businesses do not have the resources to pay individuals for these positions. Well, if you own a small business, you can work with freelancers that are willing to work passionately at lower prices. You can find these freelancers on Upwork or Freelancer.com.

Get the Pacing Right
While making efforts to be active on social media, there are specific questions you need to provide answers to. How frequently will you put

up posts on social media? Will you post once a week, or will it be more frequent?

Well, the answer to this question is dependent on the site involved. One basic rule is if you are putting up blog posts that are long, then, it is okay if you make posts weekly or twice a week. If you are posting on such sites as Instagram, LinkedIn, and Facebook, you might have to make up to five posts weekly. This is because people on these sites are used to getting regular content from various brands. You can even make more posts on Twitter. It is okay to have lots of tweets in one day. While at this, it is important to have one thing in mind. Don't just make posts for the sake of posting. Every post that you make must have some form of relevance to your target audience.

Have A Schedule, But Add Some Flexibility

As soon as you can conclude about how frequently to make posts, you must provide an answer to the question "when."

As far as posts on social media are concerned, science, as well as art, is involved. There are certain times which are regarded as perfect for posting because they are periods when people visit social media the most. Normally, people spend time on social media after work and during lunch breaks. Nonetheless, if you make posts only around these times, you will start appearing a little too robotic. This is certainly not what you want.

There are lots of tools for good content management. However, one of the best is Co-Schedule. Co-Schedule is a great WordPress plugin.

Be Authentic and Personal

Getting acquainted with people on social media can be likened to doing so in a social gathering. Just like you need to be yourself and be authentic to make friends at social gatherings, you do not have to pretend to be someone you're not on Twitter.

Always remember this while you make posts online. A lot of people might not be very comfortable getting close to a brand with a social media presence that is not flexible or that is a little too serious. You should have a personality on social media, be warm and interactive. If people find you nice and interactive, you can be certain that they will follow you.

You Should Have A Content Pipeline

A post that is funny can attract a viewer for a couple of minutes. However, if you want to ensure that your viewers keep returning to your page, you must post content that is engaging. If you can get this done, you can be sure that people will come visiting your page.

Ensure that a pipeline for your content is developed. What are the types of content you post? Where and when will they get published? You should have a plan and follow it strictly. However, if your plan is not working well, it is okay to make changes.

Mix Up Your Content Offerings

You cannot share content without having a plan. But really, what kind of content will you share? Well, to do things the right way, you should have various kinds of content. You should be able to strike a balance between your content and content curated from sites that are not yours. You should get content that will be valued by your audience but may be difficult for them to find themselves.

The content which you curate should bring a balance to those you create initially. If the content you share is only from others, it will appear that you are a parasite that takes advantage of the hard work done by others. On the other hand, if you release only content that you create yourself, you might appear like all you care about is promoting your brand. With the right balance, you can seem humble and knowledgeable.

Link, Link, And Link

Again, as soon as the social media presence of your business becomes strong, the next thing to do is get people connected to it repeatedly. You should not make this look forceful so that no one suspects cases of spamming. However, you should emphasize your brand.

The fantastic thing that businesses with more than one social media accounts enjoy is these accounts can all be linked. You can connect your twitter page to a post you put up on your blog. You can put up a photo on Instagram and tell your audience to learn more about it on your Facebook page.

Coordinate from A Central Dashboard

Having multiple accounts is excellent. There is, however, a downside. It can be quite confusing. You have decided to make a post on a particular social media account, but you are not sure which one anymore.

You may need to make use of a tool to ensure that your social media activities stay coordinated. Examples of tools that can be used to coordinate your social media activities are Sprout Social, Hootsuite, and Sensible. With any of these devices, you can have a dashboard that is centralized. Once you do this, you can view everything that is happening all over your social media platforms on a single screen. There are lots of social media management platforms. All you need to do is carry out your research and make a choice of the best one for you.

Add Value for Customers

There is an important question that is usually asked by business owners regarding making posts on social media. That question is "Once I begin interacting with customers, what approach should I take?"

The gimmick is to draw a line between getting personal with your audience and passing the message of your brand across. The aim is to have increased sales without appearing like all you want to do is market. With social media, making people aware of your brand and bringing about increased visibility at the sales funnel's top. It, however, isn't the right place to drive price points.

Your focus should be on increasing your customers' value in ways which are subtle. Give them vital tips. Provide answers to their questions and solutions to their problems. You can go as far as providing strategies which will help them do better in business. You will make more sales as soon as you begin adding value to their lives.

Make Important Business Contacts

Social media is also known as social networking. It is not known as social networking for nothing. There is a reason behind this. This reason is that the internet is the best place to make vital connections. It is important to make use of your social presence in building relationships which will be of help soon.

You can have more than one strategy to make this a reality. With LinkedIn, you can get in touch with people that could hire you in the future. LinkedIn can also help you avoid the embarrassment of gate-keepers at firms you intend doing business with. On Twitter, you can share thoughts with thought leaders of various industries. Bonding with the general public is possible on Facebook. There are lots of opportunities on social media. Take advantage of them.

Don't Be Scared of Trying New Things

For some time now, social media has passed as a productive marketing plan. We have discovered that there are special ways of doing things on social media. There are certain norms that should be adhered to. They include how frequently to post, when, and where to post.

You might follow these rules like your life depends on them initially. That is because doing so will be best for you until you have a good understanding of how things really work on social media. As soon as you understand things better, you can come up with new strategies.

Alternate the timing as well as the volume of content that you post. Put up different posts. Go into fresh social sites that are not so popular. Play around with convention. This might help you discover fresh strategies that will work well for your business.

Track Your Company's Reputation
Social media sites are ideal for putting up details concerning your business. There is, however, a secret - other people talk about your brand. This is not limited to you.

While you browse through different social sites, spend time getting to know your business's reputation. Get to discover what is being said about your brand. If you come across positive comments, show some gratitude for the good comments and promise to continue the right path. If you notice negative comments, try to fix that aspect of your brand.

Measure the Results of Social Media
Earlier in this book, we spoke about how important it is to have a goal when starting. Always have the reason you joined social media in your mind - it could be to have improved exposure or to have better sales, whatever your reason, goals are important.

As you go on, it is important that you keep setting goals to check out how much progress you have made. If an increase in sales was your goal, go through the figures. Have they increased? If better service was your target, try to find out, have you been able to make any noticeable change with your efforts on social media?

Social media is time-consuming. It also requires money and energy. You definitely do not want to skimp on any of these. Making it a habit to constantly check your results will ensure that your efforts are not in vain.

There are lots of social media sites which have several different uses. This is how to get the best out of them.

Start out with primary goals. Think about them when you come up with strategies, an identity, and your audience

Set up your presence on social media with a good volume of content. This content should come from your business, as well as other sources.

Discover new ground, experiment, and follow your success closely. With social media, your business can thrive and grow. Always remember that it will take some time.

Best Social Media Marketing/Management Tools

Social media can be frustrating if you don't have the appropriate tools or knowledge. Irrespective of what your aim is, you will need the appropriate social media marketing tools.

Below are a few that can make your social media process as seamless as possible.

Buffer

This is one of the most renowned tools for marketing on social media. It gives you the ability to schedule any kind of posts across any channel you desire. It even lets you specify a posting pattern like daily or weekly.

Buffer also gives you the opportunity to follow up on your posts, seeing which of them were most effective and why.

Sprout Social

This is a complete tool for social marketing which aims in helping managers control their efforts better. It comes with multi-level access, which allows for directional control. It also gives team members at the lower level access to allow them to better delegate and coordinate tasks.

It comes alongside an elaborate analytics platform, post scheduling abilities, and a social listening platform to aid you in a better understanding of how your demographics utilize your chosen platform.

MeetEdgar

This is a tool for scheduling on social media which lets you reuse prior posts. All you need to do is to arrange your posts and schedule content by class. Edgar then goes through and posts your content from every category. The instant it is done going through all the posts you have scheduled; it will begin recycling prior updates.

Hootsuite

This is a tool which is very simple and easy to use. Its simplicity does not compromise how powerful it can be for the average social media manager. It comes with a free version alongside budget-friendly paid options. You can utilize Hootsuite in scheduling posts beforehand on a host of diverse social channels and measure analytics to aid you in having an idea in regards as to how your content is doing.

IFTTT

This means: If this, then that'. Using this, you will be able to merge a range of tools to develop an individual group of instructions. For example, you will be able to set it up to send a tweet whenever you make a new Facebook post. It may be difficult to understand initially, but you can utilize other recipes to make it plug and play. The best part is that it does not cost anything to use.

SocialOomph

At first glance, this solution may not look as complex as a few of the apps above. However, it offers great functionality which makes it worth having a look at. With this solution, you will be able to control a mass of diverse updates at the same time. For example, you will be able to make several blog posts and save them to a text-file. Then, you can upload them to be distributed randomly at specific time-based intervals on the channels you choose. You will also be able to check out intuitive analysis tools and features to aid you in enhancing your audience's engagement.

BuzzSumo

This is another great tool which helps you discover trending, fresh or new content on the internet. With this, you can input a keyword selection or topic and locate a breakdown of some of the trending posts in those classes alongside a list of influencers who are sharing that content.

It is an amazing method of learning new ideas for your social media campaigns and content marketing. It also helps in identifying influencers in your sector who can aid in growing your visibility, reputation and following.

Feedly

This is best recognized as a tool for content discovery. This tool is a content aggregator, and you can utilize it in collecting content from any number of diverse areas, merging your perfect material into one feed that you can go through in your free time.

Although like BuzzSumo, it won't provide you with similar comprehensive metrics, but it will offer you lots of reading material, so you will always have things to post on your social media profiles.

Oktopost

This is a tool designed specifically for B2B organizations. It gives you the ability to schedule content and measure its efficiency, create content to share, and pick up social conversations that are crucial to your organization. It also aids in the management of huge social media teams.

Tagboard

This is a solution for social listening. All you need to do is include a topic, term or hashtag and you will see the discussion regarding that topic in the social scope. It is an advanced method of monitoring things like product and brand mentions, but it is also a helpful tool for generating new concepts on what you should post and how you should engage your followers especially as new trends come up.

Chapter 4:
Top Social Media Platforms

Social media is a platform open to people from various works of life. Are you a business owner, a brand ambassador, or a marketer and what have you? You can leverage the power of social media to your advantage and reach out to a larger target audience.

However, it is essential to know the various social media sites that will enable you to achieve your goals. There are different factors to consider when choosing social media sites to sign up to. Although it is necessary to be part of social media sites with a large user's base, it is more important to belong to one that best fits your business.

Does your target audience use the site? How many of these sites can you manage effectively at a time and how well does the site describe your brand? All of these are things you need to consider equally.

Below is a list of the current top social media sites. You might be familiar with some or all of them. It is advisable that you do a thorough read-through of these sites and decide on the ones that will best fit your brand.

Leading Social Media Platforms Based on The Number of Users

There are five leading social media platforms based on their number of active monthly users, and the first is none other than Facebook. Facebook leads the chart with a staggering figure of 2.2 billion active users monthly. Next in line is yet another popular network with 1.8 billion active users monthly, which is the one and only YouTube. WhatsApp and Facebook Messenger come next in line with monthly active users of 1.5 billion and 1.3 billion respectively. Instagram comes in fifth place having 1 billion active users monthly.

Surprisingly, Twitter and Snapchat didn't make it into the list of the top five as they fell into eighth and tenth positions, respectively while Kik has the lowest figure of 51 million active users monthly. The answer to these three questions will determine the social media platform that will best suit your business.

Who Is Your Target Audience?

Now and then, you may receive ads from various businesses that offer services unrelated to what you require. First, investing in such a business is a complete waste of money, and secondly, most individuals with experience would reason that such businesses need to hire a more competent person to handle their ad targeting.

Reaching out to the wrong audience will only cause you a loss of money and record little or no progress. If you find it challenging to decide the best target audience for your business, the answer to the following questions will show you a way out.

- What is the gender and average age of your target audience?

- What is the average income of your target audience?

- Where are they located?

- Who or what firms do they work for?

- Are they family people?

- Do they own a home?

- What are the challenges they face that require a solution?

- What do they love doing?

- How do they get informed, through the internet or traditional means?

With this, you have a general idea of who makes up your target market. Facebook Audience Insight comes in handy for better profiling of your target market.

Are You B2C OR B2B?
Are you a business to customer (B2C) kind of brand or business to business (B2B) kind? Because it is not yet a common thing for people to

visit social media sites whenever they want to make a purchase, it might require considerable effort to get their attention when they would rather scroll over to the next post on their feed unless they are making an impulsive purchase. However, it has been observed that active social media users are the best target market.

The best platform for B2B business where you can promote your business and reach out to the right audience are platforms such as LinkedIn. Here, you can blog about your business, share vital information that will get the attention of people and publish high-quality content.

What Are Your General Social Media Goals?

A good number of business owners, including social media marketers, do not have a clear vision of what they hope to achieve using social media. They keep emphasizing achieving goals without really knowing what their goals are. Chances are you would keep going around in circles without making any visible progress. If you must make sales on social media platforms, then it is necessary that you have a clear vision of what you wish to achieve and work towards it. Always remember that most social media platforms are sites where people go to see things and not to do things; hence, it takes more than just words but action to make a profit off it.

Below are a few social media platforms that would work correctly for both small- and large-scale businesses:

- Pinterest

- Snapchat

- Facebook

- Instagram

- Twitter

- LinkedIn

Top Social Media Platforms for Businesses Facebook

Facebook is the largest social media platform available, with over two billion individuals utilizing it monthly. This makes up a considerable part of the global population. Over 60 million organizations are utilizing Facebook pages and over five million advertisers are actively promoting their organizations on Facebook. This makes it a great option if you want to have a social media presence.

It is easy to begin on Facebook because all kinds of content function properly on Facebook ranging from videos, images, stories and text. However, you need to understand that the Facebook algorithm gives priority to content that triggers relevant interactions and conversations between individuals.

You also need to note that your content must be optimized for mobile because more than 90 percent of the users on Facebook access the application using the mobile app.

It is crucial to use Facebook if your customers belong to any of the following categories:

Seniors: Individuals who are 55 years and above. This is a popular option for this age group because it is where they can view pictures of their family and grandkids.

International markets: As opposed to other websites on social media, Facebook is used globally. It is most popular in Europe and in Middle Eastern countries. However, it is not as popular in Asia.

Small niche markets: Facebook consists of numerous groups where individuals with unique interests gather. If you have a small niche business, Facebook may be filled with groups of likely new clients.

YouTube

YouTube is a platform for sharing videos, and its users watch numerous hours of videos daily. To begin, you can create a channel on YouTube for your brand where you will be able to upload videos for your subscribers to share, like, view and comment.

Aside from being the next largest website on social media, YouTube is frequently recognized as the next biggest search engine next to Google.

Instagram

Instagram_is a social media app for sharing videos and photos. It gives you the ability to share various content like videos, photos, live videos and stories. Recently, it released IGTV for lengthier videos.

If you have a brand, you can create an Instagram business profile. This will offer you in-depth analytics of your posts and profile, and the ability to schedule posts on Instagram with the help of third-party tools. Instagram is ideal if your target market belongs to any of the following:

Millennials: The largest number of users on Instagram are individuals below the age of 25. If your target market consists of this group, Instagram is ideal for you.

Women: According to statistics, men are not as active as women on Instagram. If you sell services and products for women, this platform is the best location to advertise it.

Twitter

Twitter is a social media platform for politics, news, sports, and entertainment among others. Twitter is unique from other social media platforms in that it has a big emphasis on real-time information, which are taking place right now.

Another distinct feature of Twitter is that it supports just 280 characters per tweet as opposed to most of the platforms on social media which have a much greater limit.

Twitter is often utilized as a channel for customer service. As stated by advertisers on Twitter, over 70 percent of social customer service requests take place on Twitter.

There are numerous customer service tools for social media like Buffer Reply, which is available to aid you in managing your customer service conversations on social media.

If your potential customers belong to any of the following groups, Twitter would be a great option for your business:

Teenagers: Like Snapchat and Instagram, it is well-known among teens. Your content has a better chance of going viral among this demographic via re-tweets if it is interactive, funny or thought-provoking.

Millennials: Individuals who are a bit older than teenagers, in the early professional range or just out of college can also be found on Twitter. They took up the trend as teens when Twitter was first released and still use it actively.

LinkedIn

Now, this is more than just a job search and resume website. It has since grown into a professional social site where experts in industries network with each other, share content and develop their brand.

It has equally become an environment for organizations to establish their authority and thought leadership in their sector and draw in talent to their organization.

LinkedIn also provides opportunities for advertisement like sending personalized ads to inboxes of LinkedIn users, improving your content and showing ads beside the website.

If your target markets are in the following groups, LinkedIn is your best option:

Businesses: If you are offering B2B services, LinkedIn is a great location for promoting them. Unlike other kinds of social media, its major goal is to connect with other businesses. For this reason, companies will be in search of services and companies like yours.

High-profile individuals: Some little businesses serve high-profile individuals or executive directors. If this is you, having a profile on LinkedIn is crucial. It shows that you are a professional, serious and established, that is ready to work alongside leaders in the field.

Snapchat

This is a social media application which emphasizes the sharing of short videos and photos, also called snaps, between friends. This popularized the stories format, which eventually branched into other platforms of social media like Facebook and Instagram. Instagram seems to have disrupted the growth of Snapchat and the interest of marketers in utilizing Snapchat for their brands.

If your target market belongs to the following groups, Snapchat is a necessity:

Teenagers: Lots of other groups have not taken up Snapchat yet. Presently, the platform mainly includes individuals younger than the age of 21. So, if this is your target market, then this is an ideal choice. But if this is not the case, this platform consumes lots of time to use.

Reddit

Reddit is also recognized as the internet's front page. It is a platform where users can submit images, questions, and links. They are also able to talk about them and give them an up or down vote.

There are subreddits which cover almost anything you can think of. However, these come with various levels of engagement so it is a great idea to research them to find out if there are popular subreddits you brand can partake in.

Popular Messaging Services

Like social media platforms, there are popular messaging services you should be aware of. Some of these include:

WhatsApp

This is a messaging application utilized by individuals in more than 180 nations. At first, WhatsApp functioned for individuals as a means of communication with friends and family. But slowly, individuals began to communicate with organizations using WhatsApp.

WhatsApp has been evolving to let organizations have an appropriate profile for their business to offer customer support and distribute updates with clients regarding their purchases. For small organizations, it has developed the WhatsApp business application while large and medium businesses have the WhatsApp Business API.

Telegram

Telegram shares a lot of similarity to most of the apps for social messaging and is often recognized for the security it offers as a messaging application.

Brands can utilize it in numerous ways, aside from offering customer support. Brands can develop chatbots for Telegram or use the channel feature offered by Telegram to broadcast messages to an infinite number of subscribers.

All in all, social media is an excellent strategy for digital marketing as long as you prioritize which platforms you use. Don't try to adopt every possible form of social media; instead, do the research and think through which platforms are best for your small business's unique needs.

Chapter 5:
YouTube Marketing

If you are developing plans to start marketing on YouTube, you need to be knowledgeable about it. YouTube has over 50 million content creators producing videos frequently, so your content needs to be unique.

Another issue is reaching and keeping your main audience engaged. Most of the viewers on YouTube do not love advertising that much, so you need to carefully plan how you intend to raise awareness regarding your brand while ensuring you entertain your viewers.

This may seem daunting, but if you use the appropriate approach, it is not impossible to do. Now, before you decide to use YouTube for promoting your business, there are a few things you need to determine first.

Is YouTube Marketing the Best Solution for Your Organization?

YouTube is one of the largest websites around. Presently, it is the second most recognized website globally. And although lots of people don't consider YouTube as a search engine primarily, a lot of individuals use it for just that. YouTube is the next most-popular search engine after

Google. What this implies is that this platform offers your business tremendous opportunities.

Because YouTube is a viral platform, it also implies that the competition is enormous. As stated by Statista, YouTube has an upload of 400 hours of video every minute. So, if you desire to attain success on YouTube, you must ensure that you have the resources and time to publish high-quality content consistently. You require an excellent plan for marketing on YouTube.

Another reason that this platform is a great marketing choice is because YouTube is entirely about video. And presently, video marketing is what is trending. Videos have proven themselves continuously as one of the best forms of content marketing with regards to engagement. What is more, although you are developing them for YouTube, that does not imply that you can't use these videos for other purposes.

These videos could suit your other social media profiles. They will also be ideal for your landing pages and websites. That is not all. They can also be a great addition to your email marketing alongside any channels or platforms that you may be utilizing.

As for the problem of video production, it is not as hard as you may think to develop marketing videos. You don't require a massive budget, and you don't have to invest too much in equipment.

In summary, yes, in most situations, YouTube is a good solution for your business. If you are into the sale of products, it is a fantastic method of promoting and showcasing them and all their benefits. If you run a B2B organization, it is a tremendous platform for broadening your reach and getting more leads.

Creating A Marketing Strategy for YouTube

YouTube marketing is like marketing on other social channels. What you need to do first is to develop your strategy. To develop your strategy, you will begin by defining your objectives. Put down the precise targets you want to attain, like:

- Engagement

- Traffic/ clicks

- Subscriber Numbers

Utilize the SMART model to aid you in creating good objectives:

- Specific

- Measurable

- Attainable

- Relevant

- Time-Bound

This will aid in ensuring that your objectives have a deadline, are specific and are possible to do. Of course, you also must be able to measure your progress accurately. At this level of strategizing, determine what your key performance indicators are to aid you in measuring your outcomes.

Understand Your Audience?

You may have a correct sense of your target viewers already, but it is essential to see how they behave on YouTube. Determine if they use their hand-held devices to view videos and the type of videos they are viewing.

Search for useful tools that can help you provide answers to these questions. These tools will give you the ability to ascertain your viewers' habits. They will also give you the ability to make changes to your content.

Understand Your Brand?

If you have plans to market your brand via your channel on YouTube, it is essential that you have a clear definition of what you stand for. You need to also know the way you want to portray yourself to your audience.

Clearly state what you would want your audience to know about your products, services, and brand. Also, make sure this information is passed through your content.

Familiarize Yourself with The Competition

Invest time in viewing and researching your competitor's videos. Doing this will let you see the type of video content they are already creating, the areas they are successful in and areas you will be able to do better.

You can also use this research to attain video inspiration and develop a marketing strategy for your content on YouTube that would make you unique. If you have no idea how to locate your competitors, try searching YouTube with keywords lined with your company. Then look at the videos that relate to your field.

Point Out What Success Seems Like

Before you can create great branded videos, you must determine what success for your organization, and you look like. Is a successful video one that inspires lots of engagement from users or one that pulls in the most viewers?

You will only can create YouTube content that can meet your audience's requirements the moment you have determined what you consider a success.

Follow A Schedule

Consistency is crucial on YouTube if you want to continue growing your channel. Like blogging, the more content you place out there, the higher your chances of getting to a broader audience.

Most successful YouTubers have a rigorous schedule for publishing, and they comply with it. These YouTubers also utilize other platforms of social media in promoting new videos. This ensures that even individuals who are not subscribers of your channel will still have an idea of when new videos will be out.

When creating a YouTube marketing strategy for your organization, put into consideration how you can commit realistically to publishing new content and ensure you follow it.

The instant you have determined your posting frequency, you need to also determine when your videos will be released. Most audiences watch videos on YouTube on weekends and in the evenings. The best time for posting content is early Saturday or Sunday mornings or early afternoons during the week.

During this stage, list out all the upcoming events and holidays significant to your viewers so you will know beforehand possible moments to develop special content.

Kinds of YouTube Marketing Videos

Now that you have figured out your publishing frequency and you know what your goals are, you need to determine the kind of videos you can create on YouTube.

It is crucial to diversify things to keep your viewers entertained and heading back to your page for more. Also, it is a good idea to try out various kinds of videos early, so you know which of them works best for you and which do not.

Below are some concepts to help you begin:

Listicles

These are well-known formats for content, both as media and blog posts. You will be able to develop listicles which pinpoint your services or products such as "the five most creative methods" of using (your services). The listicle can also be informational, educational and entertaining. Don't forget, the list should always be significant to the interest of your audience and your business niche.

Behind the Scenes Videos

YouTube is a social network. One of the methods of humanizing your brand and showing that you are more than just a service or product is by sharing a few behind the scenes videos.

How-To Videos

These tend to perform well when they offer your viewers lots of value. For example, say you were into the sales of electronic devices, you could create how-to videos which show your viewers how to begin using a new device. You can check out blog posts with top performers to get material for these videos, or you can create a plan for a series.

Product Review Videos

This is a fantastic way of showcasing your own services or products. These videos can teach viewers how to utilize specific features, highlighting recent product updates or announcing your company's latest offerings.

Interviews

Interviewing popular influencers and experts in your field is another great method of drawing in new viewers. These professionals will come with their own following, so if they help you in promoting the video as well, they can aid in driving traffic to your channel on YouTube.

Case Studies

Creating video case studies of your customers is another means of promoting your business and services. These case studies don't have to be just about your products alone. They can focus on plans, recent achievements and origin stories of your clients.

How to Manage Your YouTube Channels?

After covering your YouTube marketing strategy, you will want to make an emphasis on managing your channel. Engagement is a major aspect of YouTube, so it is crucial to take time in responding to comments and in driving engagement using other methods.

A great method of managing your account is to utilize a tool to aid in automating the process. Agora pulse allows you moderate your comments in advance, respond to and view comments from the social inbox of your dashboard and observe YouTube for mentions of your brand in comments and videos.

Below are some additional YouTube tips to enhance your views and engagement:

- Go through your comments daily so you can respond promptly.

- Use monitoring to locate other mentions of your brand and find opportunities to engage.

- Ask your viewers questions in your videos. Also, ask them questions in your video descriptions to inspire them to leave comments.

- Utilize the Community tab which you can find in the main page of the channel to post video previews, GIFs, images.

HOW TO MAKE GOOD YOUTUBE VIDEOS

Begin with A Plan

Although making videos on the spot is a great choice for comedy channels, they don't tend to work well for professional ones. Before you begin to film, determine:

- What goal do you want the video to achieve?

- The audience you are targeting these videos for.

- The type of video you want to create.

- Things you will film to achieve the goals of the video.

- Who will you feature in the video?

- The video equipment you will require.

The aim here is to figure out everything and write it down before you begin to film, so that the instant you begin, you can develop the amazing video you thought of initially. The more details you can sort out in advance, the better your chances of getting your viewers intrigued.

Get the Appropriate Video Equipment

There are numerous reasons most brands choose not to create video content, but a major reason is that they believe that they require a host of fancy equipment to make everything look great. Aside from that, they believe they require an expert production crew to run the video equipment. However, the truth is, once you have decided on the kind of videos you want to produce, you will be amazed at how low-tech a few of the crucial video equipment may be.

Now, you will be able to purchase a camera that can capture 4k for a decent price and lots of smartphones today already come with an HD digital camera. Filming can be as seamless as recording a video using your smartphone or camera. You will also require some other tools like lighting, tripod, and a microphone. All of these are easy to use, inexpensive and aid in creating professional videos of high-quality.

Optimize Your Tags, Video Description and Title

The instant you have made your video and began the process of uploading it on YouTube, one of the initial things you need to do is input the video's tags, description, and title. These are the things search engine crawlers go through whenever an individual carries out a search, so it is crucial to place a lot of consideration into the video tags and keywords you utilize.

When it has to do with your description, consider this as the metadata of your video. Use this section to provide a description of what your video covers, but don't miss out on the chance to add some additional timestamps and links. If you are creating a video about best practices in dog training, don't fear adding a link to your eBook on dog training. Also, if there are specific areas you are confident your viewers would want to go back to or fast forward to, you can add a timestamp in your description to aid them in finding it quickly.

Descriptions have a limit of 5,000 characters, and while it is not a necessity to write a lengthy story, it is not a bad idea to provide your viewers, and crawlers, with extra, insightful information to go through.

When inputting video tags, it is a good idea to be honest. Even though it might be tempting to use some tags about a trending, viral subject, the additional views you get as a result of your deceit will only hurt you in the end. If your video deceives viewers into watching, they will not stay around for long, and when YouTube realizes that viewers are leaving your video within seconds, it will negatively affect your search rankings.

You can utilize numerous words in a single tag, but you are restricted to a total of 500 characters, which tends to add up fast. Treat these tags the same way you would any keyword tags on your blog and make efforts to think of all the keywords and phrases your target individuals would utilize in finding a video like yours. If your video has something that is difficult to spell, you can even utilize misspellings deliberately to draw in those searchers who are grammatically incorrect.

Utilize A Custom Image on Your Thumbnail

One of the first things individuals will see after a search is your video thumbnail image, so it is important to choose an image which not only fits the description of your video but also draws attention to it.

After uploading your video, YouTube automatically generates numerous thumbnail images utilizing parts of your video. But, if your account has proper verification and an excellent standing, you will also can upload a custom image of your choice. The instant the video has reached the end of the processing stage, you should be able to view an option to select a custom thumbnail under the section for video thumbnails. Just ensure the file is not larger than 2MB and utilize a 1280x720 resolution for the best outcome.

Requests for Likes, Comments and Subscribers

Although you may find it a bit annoying when individuals ask you to follow, share, subscribe or comment on something online, it is a strategy that has been known to work. In the world of Twitter, requesting users to retweet causes that tweet to be reposted at a much higher rate than tweets that do not. You can also expect to observe similar outcomes when requesting for comments and likes on YouTube.

Obviously, a lot of this is dependent on how great your video is and how you ask, but you will certainly be able to earn additional subscribers, likes and comments just by making a request. This can be of help because the more comments and likes your video gets, the higher the ranking will be on the search algorithms of YouTube.

YouTube stands as the most recognized platform for video hosting on the globe. Your customers, clients, and prospects are all taking advantage of this platform to look for information, which is why it is essential that you grow your presence on this platform.

YouTube Video SEO: Important Aspects
YouTube is one of the core search engines globally. This is one of the reasons why it is an appealing tool for businesses to use in promotion. Just think about what's possible reaching almost two billion users every month.

What this implies is that if you put in efforts to optimize your videos and you create videos of high-quality regularly, you can drastically enhance the possibility of you reaching a targeted and broad audience.

So, how then can you optimize your videos on YouTube?

There are a host of important elements which determine your social results ranking. A few of them are totally under your control. Some of these include the keywords you utilize and how you utilize them. However, there are other areas you can't exercise control over like how many individuals instantly subscribe after checking out one of your videos.

Below are some crucial ranking factors for videos that you should be aware of. They include:

The Keywords of Your Channel
Utilize the appropriate tags to ensure that YouTube can tell what your channel is offering.

Video Descriptions and Headlines
Research keywords to point out what your audience is searching for and utilize these keywords in your video descriptions and headlines. Note that, the nearer the keyword is to the start of the headline, the better.

Video Transcript
Adding a video transcript is a fantastic method of ensuring search bots can scrape your videos. It is also perfect for viewers because if they need to check a word's spelling or are unable to hear a video, they will still be able to follow your content.

Watch Time

Your overall video watch time also has an impact on your ranking. The higher the watch time, the better the effect it will have.

Video Tags

Asides from keywords, you must include tags in your videos. To determine the ones that will perform best, you should do proper research beforehand.

Thumbnail Image

This image can be seen anytime your video is indexed. So, you need to ensure it is relevant and compelling.

Number of Subscribers

This has to do with the number of subscribers you have on YouTube. As stated earlier, the amount of people subscribing after checking out one of your videos is also crucial. These subscribers prove that your video was useful to the viewer and offered value.

Marketing Success on YouTube

If you use it the right way, YouTube can be an excellent method of reaching more potential clients and promoting the awareness of your brand. You can ensure your strategy for marketing on YouTube is heading towards success by beginning with these core steps:

- Create a strategy for your YouTube presence beforehand and plan your videos ahead to ensure you regularly publish new content.

- Create various kinds of videos to appeal to a broader audience.

- Put in the effort with each new video to engage with your viewers and subscribers.

- Optimize your videos and channel for YouTube's search engine to improve your reach.

Chapter 6:
Facebook Marketing

Facebook is one of the leading platforms of social media in the world. For this reason, marketing on Facebook has transformed into one of the largest digital channels regarding new opportunities. The platform provides a range of different organic and paid tools which brands can use in putting themselves in front of Facebook's growing user base. Just like any other digital platform, there are a few things you must do if you want to exploit Facebook to gain more leads. Now, let us read on to find out a few of the fundamentals of Facebook Marketing.

Are Your Target Viewers on Facebook?

Before you take the first step and begin checking out strategies for marketing on Facebook, you need to first answer this question - are your target viewers on Facebook?

The answer is most likely.

According to new data, it has been proven that individuals of all ages utilize at least one form of social networking. Younger individuals had the most percentages. Also, women and men use social media in equal proportion.

Additionally, when it has to do with the platform individuals utilize, Facebook is at the top of the list. As of January 2018, 68 percent of Americans utilized Facebook, while Instagram was next with 35 percent.

Irrespective of the age group your target viewers fall in, you will find more users than you need on Facebook.

Now that we have covered this, let us move on to how you begin using Facebook for your promotion.

BUILDING YOUR BRAND ON FACEBOOK

How Can Facebook Aid in Building Your Brand?
The mistake lots of businesses make is assuming that social media platforms, especially Facebook, are just avenues to broadcast the message of your brand to the large number of individuals who utilize the platform. When this fails, lots of these organizations, don't go any further and assume that Facebook does not function for them.

The issue is that this is not the function of Facebook. Individuals do not go on social media platforms to hear you make presentations regarding your business. They don't want boring pitches. Many people go on social media to engage with their friends and the brands they love.

Lots of clients today appreciate brands that make efforts to get to know them on an individual level as opposed to behaving as an impersonal corporation.

Facebook can aid in building your brand by playing the role of an avenue to engage your followers. Offer solutions to their questions and get to know their requirements. When you do this, you develop your brand and inspire brand loyalty.

How Do You Develop A Community on Facebook?

Invite individuals to follow your page on Facebook. Promote your page using numerous platforms which include your newsletters, website, and emails.

Inspire the followers you must engage with your content. When your followers share or like the content you have, it will show up on news-feeds which all their connections will see as well. This then enhances your exposure and urges more individuals to like your page.

Interact with your followers. Pay attention to the website and promptly respond to their comments and questions. Ask them questions and partake in conversations that show up on your page. Ensure you do not take over the content but instead participate in enhancing engagement.

Why You Should Not Purchase Facebook Likes

If page likes are essential to mastering Facebook marketing, it brings up a valid question: why not just purchase them?

This is a serious issue for lots of people and for others it may seem like an easy and fast way of making your brand look reputable and credible.

Well, the problem is in where these likes come from. Organizations selling likes use fake accounts, click farms or even accounts that have been compromised to get the promised numbers. This implies that there is a low probability of any of these individuals who have liked your page engaging with your content.

Note that, not every post on Facebook comes up on the Newsfeed. When Facebook determines what to add, the algorithm checks out engagement rates precisely. Over time, the absence of comments and likes on your posts due to fake fans in comparison to the number of your overall Page likes, could result in your content not being shown. The average user will equally query your credibility with such differences.

If the future impacts of poor rates of engagement are not adequate to set you straight, note that Facebook has a team that looks out for this kind of distrustful behavior and they will close your page without any form of warning.

How to Create a Facebook Business Page?

If you've decided to create a Facebook page for your business, then you are on the right path. You will become a part of over 50 million businesses globally who are already marketing on Facebook through a page.

Before heading into content publishing and boosting posts via advertising, you need to learn the basics.

Create a Page on Facebook

First, there is one major area to clarify. As you must be aware, most of Facebook consists of personal profiles. But, if you are a business trying to establish your social network presence, you will have to develop a page instead.

Pages are the same as business profiles on Facebook. Pages look like profile pages, but they show precise information only applicable to causes, organizations, and businesses. To connect with a profile, you need to add them as a friend, but when it comes to a business page, you connect by liking the page and becoming a fan. If you make a personal profile for your business as opposed to a page, you have the tendency of Facebook shutting you down.

To begin creating your own page on Facebook, head to https://www.facebook.com/pages/create/. There, you will have the option of choosing from six diverse categories. They are:

- Local Place or Business

- Organization, Institution or Company

- Product or Brand

- Entertainment

- Community or Cause

- Band, Artist or Public Figure

Depending on the option you decide to go with, you will be able to customize the about fields on your page. Wisely select the name of your page. Facebook will allow you to change your URL and name in numerous situations, but it can be a tedious and challenging process.

If you have not done so yet, at this moment, you will be urged to sign into Facebook. To develop a page, you must manage it using your personal account. But your personal information won't show up on the page except if you include it.

Click on Get Started, and you be redirected automatically to your new page. Before sharing with others, Facebook will offer you four building tips for your business page foundation.

Include A Profile Picture

The initial step to providing your Facebook Page with an identity is including a profile picture. This will act as your core Page visual. It will show up in search results along with any of your content that shows up in the news feeds of your users.

Lots of publishers suggest that you create a photo that has a size of 180 x 180 pixels. But, slightly increasing this will aid in maintaining quality, if you fail to upload an image that is square already, you will be asked to crop.

Consider your profile picture as your initial impression and be sure to select something instantly recognizable. If you are a public figure, your best headshot is ideal. Shops or local restaurants may go with an image of their most recognized offering.

Include A Cover Photo

Next, Facebook will request you include a cover photo. This is a vast horizontal image that spans across the top of your page. It should show the identity of your page, and you can update it depending on campaigns, seasons or unique offerings.

To include a cover photo, select the Add a Cover Photo option. The cover photo should have a standard dimension of 851 x 315 pixels. But, if the image is not exact, you will have the option of dragging to reposition the image. Then click save.

To replace your cover photo later, move your mouse over the white camera in the lower right part of your cover image and choose Change Cover. It is also ideal to add a link in the description or a sentence of text if you are advertising a campaign. In doing this, if your cover photo highlights a new product, they can seamlessly head to your product line to purchase.

It can be challenging to find the appropriate balance between a cover photo that is both simple and visual. Try using an abstract pattern or image to draw appeal, or a landscape shot using your product as the core point. Most times, the top cover photos are those that exploit negative space.

Include A Brief Description

A short description is crucial in letting your audience know what you are offering. To begin, all you need to do is select Add a Short Description. You can find it on the welcome menu. Include 155 characters relating to your business. This description will show up both on your search results and page, so ensure it is concise but descriptive. However, don't fear showing some of the personality of your brand.

As an alternative, you will be able to edit your description by selecting 'About' in the left menu. There you will also see the option to add a website, phone number, mission, email and more.

Make A Username for Your Page

The final step on the welcome menu is to develop a username for your page. Your username will show up in your vanity URL or custom Facebook URL to aid individuals in quickly locating and remembering your page. You will be provided with 50 characters to create a name that is not being utilized by another organization.

Create Roles

After the basics, there is a crucial step you need to take before sending the page out to anyone. Remember that Facebook makes business pages unique from standard profiles? One importance of this is that numerous individuals from a company will be able to edit and post via a page without having to share login information. However, this implies you need to elect individuals with various levels of editing access. Page roles become useful here. Above the navigation bar, find 'Settings.'

Then look for 'Page Roles' in the navigation bar on the left. After adding a collaborator, you will have some options for roles which are:

Admin
Can manage all parts of the page. This means they will be able to publish as the page, send messages, delete or respond to comments, produce ads, assign page roles, see the admin who published a post among others. This individual will have similar authority as the individual who created the page, so select wisely.

Editor
They possess similar permissions as admins aside from one major difference. They will be unable to assign page roles to other individuals.

Moderator
These individuals are unable to publish as the page. However, they will be able to send and respond to messages. They will also can delete comments and create ads.

Advertiser

Can develop ads and view insights.

Analyst

They do not have any power to publish, but they will be able to see the admin who published specific posts and view insights.

Live Contributor

If you want to try out Facebook later, the live contributor option will be of help. They will be able to go live from their devices to the page. However, they will be unable to create ads, leave comments, view insights or be able to use any other tools for publishing.

Include A CTA

One of the major significances of creating a business Facebook page is the ability to draw in an audience that you may have been unable to reach if you were using a normal website. Beginning in December 2014, Facebook let pages add a Call-to-action button above the page. Select the Add a Button option on the top of your cover photo to add it.

You will be able to select from a host of options depending on what you need the viewer to do. This could either be to download an application, get in touch, book a service, donate, make a purchase or just get more information.

Verify Your Page

There is a high possibility that you have observed a blue check or tiny gray mark close to the names of a few brands and businesses.

If you classified your page as a company, local business or organization, you could be qualified for a verification badge. This is not compulsory, but it helps in giving your page a sense of authority. This could be specifically crucial for organizations in online services or e-commerce searching to develop trust with possible clients or carry out transactions online.

You could be qualified if you are an admin and your page have a cover photo and profile picture. Head to 'Settings' above your page and find your way to 'General' in the navigation menu on the left. There you will see 'Page Verification' where you will be able to enter your country, publicly listed phone number and language. A Facebook rep will reach out to you with a code for verification.

The blue check badge is only offered to a few celebrities, public figures, and brands. Sadly, you can't request this badge.

How Can You Utilize This Community in Developing Your Brand?

The instant you have a well-known community on Facebook, you need to utilize this group in growing your base and enhancing conversions. You can do this via the following:

First, provide giveaways and unique codes exclusive to your followers on social media.

Secondly, host contests where individuals get coupons which they get for telling stories about the experience they had with your brand or posting images of themselves alongside your product. This inspires individuals to purchase something else while you also spread the reach of your brand via the posts of the participants.

Thirdly, provide inside information about how to get the best out of services or products in your industry. Transform your Facebook page into a significant resource for individuals.

Fourthly, Facebook can be a treasured resource, but it is not just an amplifier for enhancing your message. Utilize this platform in building your brand, and you will find out why social media is popular as a marketing tool.

Making Your Facebook Page SEO Optimized

Your Facebook page is where you begin your marketing efforts on Facebook. Preferably, you want it to be ranking on both Facebook and Google search for your brand name to ensure your prospects and customers can find you with ease.

Then, the instant they have located your page, it should be enticing so individuals will decide to like it. The following are some best practices that can aid you in optimizing your page for both requirements:

Select A Memorable and Descriptive Username

The username of your Facebook page is sometimes referred to as a vanity URL. It is your page's web address. Typically, your page gets a random URL which comprises of numbers. Your username should convey the subject of your business name or page. This is to ensure customers and search engines can locate you in Facebook search and Google. To claim a vanity URL, you must have no less than 25 likes.

Ensure Your About Section Contains Descriptive Keywords

You're about section is your page's core real estate showing text. Ensure it describes your products and business accurately by utilizing what customers are likely to use in search queries. Ensure you add the URL of your website in your description to boost clicks through to it.

Make Sure You Utilize the Right Category for Your Organization

Lots of businesses tend to set their category inaccurately. It can pose a severe issue especially if you need to come up in Facebook's graph search. If your business is a local one, it is important that you pick it as a business type. This is because it will let individuals "check in" at your business. If your business does not have walk-in traffic and doesn't have a use for 'check-ins,' it may be better to select 'Companies & Organizations'.

Optimize the Images on Your Page

Your profile and cover photos are the first things visitors will see when they get to your page. You should have images of professional quality, which should correctly show the feel and look of your brand. Make certain they meet the recommended size requirements, so they don't seem lopsided. The image on your profile should be 160x160 pixels while your cover image should be 851x315 pixels.

Take Advantage of Pinned Posts

Typically, many individuals will only check out your page once. They will like your page and then keep interacting with your posts that show up in their newsfeed but are less likely to check out your wall. Due to this, the main function of your page is to draw people to like your page. Facebook gives admins the ability to pin a post above their page. Make sure this post has a subject that is unique, relevant and has an appealing image.

Utilizing Facebook Groups to Interact with Your Target Market

Although pages are the main tool owners of businesses should be utilizing in marketing their businesses on Facebook, a very efficient add-on strategy in lots of niches and industries are groups. When you use them the right way, groups can be a great traffic source and can result in enhanced authority and engagement for your business.

When you take part in groups owned by other people related to your industry, you will be able to aid in establishing yourself as an expert in your industry. Providing relevant tips and advice can aid you in becoming a relevant member of the group. Also, as individuals learn to trust you, they will want to learn more about your business and you.

However, probably the most valuable utilization of Facebook groups is to create and take part in your groups. Groups offer you the chance to interact with your audience in a more relatable and personal way and let you become a part of the daily conversations of your target market.

Develop a group that allows conversation about any subject that relates to your field. For example, if you are a public speaker, you could begin a group where individuals can discuss or ask questions related to public speaking.

Urging Social Sharing Via the Utilization of Facebook Plugins and Buttons

Your Facebook page and website should seamlessly work together. Often, your marketing funnel will function at pushing traffic from your page on Facebook to your blog or website. But you will always want to ensure you provide your website visitors with a means of sharing or liking your Facebook content. You also want to offer them a means of interacting with your page.

Make sure every piece of content on your website has a share and like button beside it. You will be able to manually add this or utilize a third-party service such as a WordPress plugin to customize your buttons and make the process of adding them seamless.

To offer visitors to your website the opportunity to interact with your page and like it, install the page plugin in your website's sidebar. It is also a good idea to select 'Show Page Posts' to enable visitors to your website to see a preview of the kind of content you normally share on your page.

Getting More of Your Fans to See Your Posts

Lots of page owners typically complain that many of their fans don't see their posts on Facebook. This concern has been addressed by Facebook and they have stated that the inability to see your posts is due to two core factors. Firstly, due to the huge amount of content individuals share daily, there is typically not enough room on newsfeeds of users to display every single post. This leads to a fierce competition for placements in the feeds of users and leads to minimized exposure for organic posts.

The other reason why the reach of your posts has been reduced is because Facebook's algorithm is designed to show users the most relevant content. To determine relevance, there are a host of factors that come into play, including:

- The way a person has interacted with the posts of a page previously in terms of shares, comments, and likes.

- The kind of posts being shared such as video, images, etc.

- The popularity of the previous posts of a page among every user.

The more popularity your posts have, the more they will come up in user's feeds.

To offer yourself the best opportunity of getting it into the feeds of your fans, utilize the strategies below for your organic posts:

Use more videos in your posting strategy. As stated by research, in terms of organic reach, videos are at the top.

Consult your page insights regularly to view the kinds of content your audience loves. Your page insights consist of a vast amount of data on the kinds of content your audience tend to engage with. View the post formats that are drawing in people the most, whether it be links, images, text-only posts or videos. Also, check out the topics your audience seems to enjoy. Also find out the best times, dates and frequency for posting that suits your fans.

When you post promotional content, ensure you add engaging and relevant backstory for the best reach. In 2014, Facebook announced that they would be restricting the reach of posts they deemed "too promotional". These include posts that urged people to enter a contest, purchase a product or posts that recycled content from ads.

To offer your promotional posts the best opportunity of being viewed, ensure you offer content, which is engaging, as opposed to a plea to visit your website or purchase a product.

Always ask yourself if your audience would find a post entertaining enough to read and interact with it even if they have no plans of purchasing your product.

How Often and When to Post

Lots of people who want to post on Facebook always aim to post at the right time on the right day to get peak engagement and reach. But there is no single approach which works for all instances when it has to do with the timing of posts. There has been a lot of research done on the best posting frequency and time, but it is best to utilize this as a starting location for your research. Ensure you check out Facebook insights to find out if these best practices work with your audience.

According to suggestions from research, you might get higher engagement when you post on Thursdays and Fridays. Ideal times for posting may differ significantly but posting between 1 pm and 3 pm are great times to begin your testing.

Regarding the frequency of posting, you need to find the middle-ground between informative and annoying. Some brands have been successful in posting 4-10 times daily. For others, once daily or twice a week is ideal. If you post less than two posts weekly, you will not be able to adequately engage your audience for them to retain a social connection with your brand which will cause you to lose their engagement. As a brand, posting more than twice daily can have the same result. What this means is that the right number falls around 5-10 posts weekly if you are a brand and if you are a media company it could be as much as ten times more. This is because news is information individuals tend to engage with every hour of the day.

Utilizing Paid Options to Enhance Reach and Likes

While it is not impossible to get a considerable amount of reach for your posts with the help of free strategies, you may want to use paid options to support your organic strategy. Presently, Facebook utilizes two main options for extending your page posts reach. They are:

Post Boosts

When you boost a post, it will enhance its visibility in the newsfeeds of your users. You can decide to have your posts displayed to the fans of your page, friends of your fans or other individuals who you pick via targeting. Options for the targeting of your posts consist of location, age, and gender. If you want to boost a post, all you must do is select 'Boost' when developing a new post. This setting is also available on previous posts if you need to repost a post that you have published before.

Promoted Posts

You can access promoted posts through your Facebook Ads Manager. To start developing a promoted post, head to the Ad Creator and select Boost your posts. Remember that while this still goes by the name 'Boosting,' you will have more options for budgeting and targeting than just selecting 'Boost' from your page.

Boosting posts is an easy and fast method of extending your post reach, but you can also try promoting your posts as it is an ideal option. Although it is a bit more complex to develop a promoted post, the added control, and targeting of promoted posts usually ensure, they are worth the additional effort.

Chapter 7:
Twitter Marketing

With over 300 million active users monthly alongside a young demographic, Twitter is an amazing platform for lots of marketers.

Beginning a Twitter page for your organization is very straightforward. Anybody can create a twitter handle, fill out their bio, upload their profile image and send out their initial tweet. However, the not so easy aspect of Twitter is to grow your account and transform it into a tool that grows your brand and generates leads.

Growing a real Twitter following requires more than just sending tweets any time your organization is releasing a product or has an event coming up. It also has to do with engaging and interacting with your target audience. Twitter is a very strong tool for marketing. If you can become an expert with this quick-paced site for social networking, you will discover new opportunities to develop your business online.

Why Is Twitter Different
It is not a great idea to use the same approach on all social media platforms. For example, the marketing strategy you use on Twitter is not

going to be the same as your Instagram or Facebook marketing strategies. Knowing the way Twitter works and where it fits in in the landscape of social media will determine how you utilize it. Some of the major methods organizations use Twitter include:

- Distributing content and information

- Engaging with customers

- Branding

- Networking

- Management of Reputation

- Pushing Engagement for promotional activities

As you can observe, most of these activities consist of interactions. As opposed to Pinterest or Instagram, it does not necessarily have to do with just broadcasting your content. Twitter feeds off communication.

Now that we have covered the basics let us check a few marketing strategies that you can use on Twitter which will aid you in attaining success.

Steps in Incorporating Twitter into Your Marketing Strategy

It is crucial to determine what you aim to achieve before you plan your Twitter marketing strategy. If you need to get more individuals to check out your content, your objectives should consist of some of these:

- Get leads from Twitter by urging followers to check out your landing page.

- Develop awareness for an upcoming service or product by utilizing Twitter to advertise to relevant leads.

- Develop a positive opinion regarding your services, products, and brands by utilizing Twitter as a tool for PR.

- Offer customer support via one-on-one interactions and relevant content which aids customers in getting the best out of your service or product.

- Develop a community of people with like minds to offer your ideas to innovate a service, product or entire marketing strategy.

- Develop through leadership, interact with like-minded individuals and share your thoughts.

Determine Where Twitter Can Fit into Your Marketing Strategy

Your Twitter plan will possess its own distinct identity in your strategy for content marketing. For example, a few of the things your Twitter strategy may push for are:

Conversions: you may be utilizing Twitter for integrated messaging. This is where you are looking to get a specific action such as an enrollment, subscription or signup.

Traffic: Twitter could be a means of driving traffic to your blog. You could also utilize direct links to landing pages and posts.

Sales: where any kind of tweet, whether blog posts, images, or video have just one aim - which is to enhance sales.

Point Out Your Target Audience

Targeting your audience via Twitter is not easy but very important. But there are lots of ways to locate it, making it less difficult to connect with targeted followers you can advertise your content to.

You also can develop Twitter lists for each section of your audience to monitor who like that content. Below is how you can build targeted lists of individuals you can engage with:

Search Bios for Keywords. There are tools which allow you to search for a user's bio using the target keyword of your content. You are also able to search by location.

Check out Hashtags: Use hashtags relevant to your industry and go through their streams to locate other individuals utilizing them. A session of brainstorming will direct you to the leading hashtags for your marketing objectives.

Follow and Engage: Utilize Twitter list tools such as Tweetdeck or Hootsuite to import your Twitter lists. It will make it less difficult to follow your lists and grow relationships with their members.

Decide on The Best Moments to Tweet

Not everyone is online 24/7. You must determine the periods your followers are online, and that is the ideal time to tweet.

Some things to place into consideration include your location and if your followers are on Twitter at night or during the day among others.

Below are a few tools which can help you decide the best periods to tweet to get peak engagement:

Social Bro. This helps in analyzing your followers' timelines and produces a report that will let you know when you should be tweeting to reach them.

Tweriod: Tweriod will also run a follower's analysis and let you know when they are online alongside the best periods for you to tweet. You will also be able to import these times to your buffer schedule.

Hootsuite Auto Schedule: If you use this tool, this feature will already be aware of the periods of the day your tweets get peak engagement.

Ensure Your Tweets Are Conversational

Most brands tweet in a one-dimensional manner. Their tweets are broadcasts which is not what Twitter is for. Your Tweets should not only be inspirational quotes or headlines with a link or funny statements. They should make way for conversation and communication.

Lots of reputable organizations on Twitter now reply to their customers as opposed to just broadcasting. Below are a few tips that can aid you:

- Tweet questions

- Make sure that no less than 40 percent of your tweets are replies to other individuals.

- When you tweet links, include a line consisting of your opinion to ignite conversation.

- Tweet to your audience directly - as opposed to adding a Blog Post Title and a link, you can instead write: Want to lose weight? Check out this new post: "Blog Post Title (link)"

When you are more conversational, it means an increase in engagement, which also leads to more activity to your account on Twitter in the future. Also, when you are responsive and reply to questions from your audience, it could lead to new customers.

Get Ideas for Your Content

For lots of individuals looking to market their content or services, Twitter is the leading location to find some of the leading ideas for topics. If you're thinking about your next topic or blog post, you can utilize these strategies:

Input Keywords: Input the keywords most relevant to your sector and find out what individuals are talking about. There could be many articles, discussions and a host of others that are taking place right under you. These will let you know what your target audience requires, what is trending, what influencers are talking, etc.

Follow Your Network: Your fans are tweeting about your sector, and they could offer you some relevant ideas. For example, if you see individuals asking numerous questions about a specific strategy for social media, you could write something about it.

Search for Pain Areas: Your prospective clients have issues and questions. They may be engaging on Twitter to find solutions. Keep abreast with things that are occurring to know the questions to respond to.

Select What You Share

There is a host of content on Twitter you can share aside from just text. The platform supports a range of media formats which you can embed directly in your tweet. Some of these include:

Text: These best suit tweets for news, updates, quick facts and asking your followers questions.

Video: Videos are very powerful. If you integrate it in your message, it could help in working wonders by pushing your message in front of the right audience. Include brief but entertaining videos your followers may find useful.

Images: Utilize a picture to enhance your message. It will aid in giving your tweet more impact. Photos stand out better and will help you get more engagement and impressions on your content.

Links: If you have a piece of content which is valuable and is on another platform you can't embed it, although a typical link will work. Include a hashtag to enhance its reach and provide an accurate idea of what the link is heading towards.

Slideshare: Is great for visual data. With the help of slide decks, you will be able to present lots of content in a manner that is easy to digest.

Promoting Your Content

If you use Twitter properly, you can pull in lots of traffic to your site. But, just tweeting your blog post title and a link to your site every time may not give you the results you desire.

You need a bit of creativity when creating tweets to promote your videos, blog posts, and other content. Below are a few ways of getting additional clicks on your tweets:

Leave It Brief: Tweets that do not have more than 100 characters tend to get more conversion. When you are trying to promote something, all you need to do is write a short intro which is adequate for the viewer to know what is waiting for them when they click.

Add Statistics: Individuals love figures and statistics. Utilize Twitter stats that support the argument you are trying to make. It also aids in adding validity to your content.

Add Teasers: Try adding a teaser quote to your tweet. The quote must be accurate and give the users a great idea of what to expect from the post.

Take Advantage of Hashtags: #hashtags are a good way of reaching individuals in your industry that you are not presently following. Use popular industry hashtags to do this. You can also use branded hashtags and inspire others to use it too.

Utilize Mentions: If your post mentions any industry influencers or publications, make sure you mention (@) them when promoting. If the content is good enough, there is a high chance they will also share it. This will help you reach their audience.

Request for A Share: If you want retweets, this is a great practice. All you must do is ask your audience to aid you in retweeting a post. Tweets requesting for RTs have a higher tendency of obtaining them.

Promote Your Tweets: If you are looking to get more exposure, then Promoted Tweets will help in attaining it. With just a little investment on your part, you will be able to achieve this. They are not difficult to create and can aid in bringing you a huge amount of traffic.

Creating A Tweeting Schedule

You need to have a scheduled time for posting tweets on Twitter. Your schedule for tweeting should show what you plan on tweeting and when. Your strategy should put down things like when you will be tweeting links to your new posts alongside other updates.

It's a good idea to add this into your total content strategy, especially if you tend to publish content across numerous platforms such as YouTube, a blog, etc. A major benefit of having a tweeting strategy in place is that you can avert errors like just tweeting links to recent blog posts once. Generally, this is one of the major errors brands on social media make, but it is especially worse on Twitter.

The issue with tweeting links to your content out just once is that lots of people won't see it. You must give your tweets time intervals to enhance their visibility, and to make sure that as many individuals as possible can view your content. The next question would be when should I tweet? You need to find out when your audience is most active and spread your tweets within those periods. This will ensure there is a higher possibility of people seeing your Tweets.

Set Milestones and Goals

If you don't have measurable goals you want to reach, your marketing strategy is missing a crucial factor. In the absence of milestones, goals, and objectives, you have a higher tendency of making similar errors many marketers and businesses make with marketing on social media.

Crushing It with Social Media Marketing

Lots of businesses don't exactly know if their efforts on social media are functioning or not. A big reason behind this is that organizations do not monitor their activities and neither have they set any objectives for what they intend to achieve on Twitter.

Instead, organizations just send out content and hope something will happen to enhance their brand. The strategy of publishing and hoping is not enough. First, you will have to set some goals and objectives on Twitter such as:

- Develop an engaged audience

- Monitor and enhance the reputation of your brands

- Respond to the complaints of your customers faster

- Draw more traffic to your site

- Generate Leads

- Network with influencers and bloggers

Next, you will create accomplishments that go alongside those objectives such as:

- Enhance Retweets and Mentions by 20 percent

- Keep your rate of response higher than 90 percent

- Ensure your answer is not more than 10 minutes

- Generate no more than 10 leads from Twitter monthly

- Increase traffic from referrals on Twitter by 30 percent

Ideally, all goals should come with a stated deadline. This could be monthly, weekly or quarterly or whatever works best for your organization. Utilize website analytic tools like Google Analytics and a social management tool to measure your activity and monitor the progress of your goals.

If you follow these steps, you will go further than just creating a Twitter account and following random individuals hoping you get a follow back. Try to emphasize utilizing Twitter to engage and develop your brand.

Verify Your Account – Why You Should Verify

If you have a verified Twitter account, it separates your brand or organization from the shady ones that have been created and offers you credibility. However, you need to meet specific criteria when applying for verification. These are:

Ensure Your Profile Is Updated

You need to ensure all your profile information is updated and accurate. This consists of your header picture, profile picture and bio.

Phone and Email Verification

Next, you must confirm and verify your email address and phone number. You can find the options to do both of this in the Settings and Privacy option.

Let Your Tweets Be Public

To get a verified account on Twitter, you need to set your tweets to public. Next, ensure your profile has to do with your business. This implies that having a stock image on your handle could prevent you from getting verification.

Apply for Verification

The instant your profile is ready, you will be able to apply for verification via the request verification form on Twitter. Ensure you make available any supporting documents or URLs of websites that could aid your cause in your respective industry.

If you are trying to verify a personal account, you may need to submit an ID card issued by the government. Then a group of moderators will aid in reviewing your profile before a decision is made. If your verification request is not approved the first time, you are able to apply again after 30 days.

Chapter 8:
Instagram Marketing

It did not appear like Instagram was anything special when it first made its way into the social media scene in 2010. Instagram had a lot in common with the then available social media platforms. It contained pictures of different foods, pets, and selfies.

Eight years after 2010, Instagram is no longer a platform for just posting pictures. It is now a tool for carrying out full-scale marketing.

When a look is taken at a log of the latest features on this platform, it is evident that lots of instruments that are beneficial to businesses have been added to Instagram in the last 12 months. Some of these tools are fresh methods of pushing traffic on Instagram, advanced analytics, and Instagram posts that are shoppable.

It doesn't matter what sector of the economy you find yourself in, you will not regret having a strong Instagram presence. However, if you must get in front of others, it is vital that you have a perfect understanding of Instagram, as well as your target audience on this app. You should also know the types of content that generate the most views, how to get your KPIs and metrics tracked, and how to have a strategy for Instagram stories.

Why Instagram Marketing Is Key to Ecommerce Success

Virtually everyone is aware of how amazing it is to share videos and photos with friends and loved ones on Instagram. That, however, is not all that Instagram is about. It is an excellent tool for e-commerce.

Why is this so? Well, the simple reason for this is that Instagram has a very visual format. As a result of this, it offers lots of opportunities to e-commerce businesses that are interested in showing off what they have. This can be done through Instagram stories, videos, and photos. Lots of businesses are now aware that a strong presence on Instagram is an excellent complement for e-commerce marketing.

Tips for Instagram Marketing That You Should Know

Optimize Your Bio

In addition to your username, website URL, and business name, there are 150 characters offered by your Instagram profile for inputting your bio.

Your bio gives you the privilege of making a first impression. It is also a chance to tell people about your business. With your bio, you should be able to tell people who you are, as well as the services you offer. This is in addition to giving out information about the Identity of Your

Brand. With just 150 characters, doing this might not be so easy. This, therefore, makes it vital that you have a copy that is:

- CLEAR: Make use of simple and short words. Also, your texts should have line breaks.

- CONCISE: Emojis can help you develop a personality for your brand.

- COMPELLING: With a call to action, it is very easy to let visitors know their next line of action.

Select the Right Profile Picture

Your profile picture creates a first impression. Visitors to your page notice it before going on to your bio. As a result of this, a business Instagram account will have to make use of its logo as its profile picture. Every logo must be untouched by the circle which Instagram is known for. It should also be clear. By zooming out, you can fix a logo that has a square appearance.

Build Consistent Instagram Aesthetics

If there's one thing that's difficult about making your Instagram feed have a great look, it's getting your pictures to look good when placed together. It is essential to look beyond just posting a picture and look at your entire Instagram feed - how do your photos look beside each other? These tips should help

Select A Color Scheme

Having a steady color scheme meant just for Instagram feeds is important. The result of this is there will be an effortless blend between the colors throughout your feed. You may decide to make your feed warm and comfortable, cool and dark, or colorful and bright.

Irrespective of what combination you intend using, with a color palette that is consistent, it becomes easy to add branding to your Instagram feeds.

Focus on Lighting

As far as aesthetics and duration are concerned, lighting is of the utmost importance. Picture any upscale magazine that you enjoy reading. Irrespective of what is being discussed - the choice of colors, as well as the lighting are key attractions. Your Instagram should maintain a consistency in these areas for a more pleasing aesthetic.

Your Goals Should Be Clearly Defined

In the absence of any created goals, there will be no way to tell if your investment in Instagram marketing is yielding a profit. The first step in the creation of goals is selecting the best yardstick for gauging success. This falls into two classes:

- "Vanity" metrics (shares, likes, followers, comments)

- "Business" metrics (traffic, revenue-gen, engagement, reach)

With vanity metrics, you can estimate how your content is faring and how your audience view your content. With vanity metrics, you can also know how competitive your presence is on Instagram.

Business metrics will give you a view of social media's contribution to business in the big picture. They are both important in different ways. Also, they must be considered before setting up a Business Instagram.

Create Engaging Content

Engaging content attracts an audience. It drives people to share, click, and comment. You cannot get an individual to take any action if you can't get them to give you attention. There are lots of methods which will get people's attention and focus. Some of them are:

Behind the Scene Shots

This content format is used to introduce the individuals that serve as your business's backbone. With behind the scene videos and images, the humane side of your brand is revealed. This makes followers realize that collaboration has a role to play in driving your business.

It is also okay to make posts that publicize the profile of some of your executives, show employees at work, and show what your office looks like. Whatever helps outsiders have an idea of what is going on inside.

Space Out Your Content

This can be the most challenging part of creating an attractive Instagram feed. It is important that you are aware of just where each photo should be, as well as how to have a planned feed that helps all photos blend together.

Your aim should be to develop a depth of field, just like in the case of photography. You might need to separate busy photos from each other and keep them closer to minimal photos to get the right balance.

Keep Things Consistent

To ensure that your feeds have a natural flow, it is vital that you take the right approach when correcting your photos. The implication of this is that you can't work with just one filter. However, making use of just a few filters will be great.

Do you like warmer tones? Regardless of what style you use in editing, ensure there is a consistency that will let you maintain a good flow. The use of just a tinge of one filter style can help your brand in more ways that you are aware of.

Quotes and Text-Based Images

A lot of people enjoy going through quotes that they have a good understanding of. This, therefore, makes quotes a tremendous and relatively effortless way to build engagement. You should develop text-based material that takes advantages of:

- Quotes made by people of influence in your industry

- Facts that are specific to an industry

- Satisfies customer reviews

Daily Hashtags

With daily hashtags, it is easy to streamline your content. This can also help you develop a theme which can keep your audience expectant. It also plays a role in helping you come up with ideas.

Try developing some classy hashtags. An example of this is #tbt (Throwback Thursday), which is known by lots of people. You can also go ahead and develop something entirely new. It could be related to the business you are involved in.

Master the Little-Known Features and Hacks

Are you aware that it is possible to:

- Alter the color of fonts, as well as words so your text can be unique?

- Hide your story from specific individuals?

- Include line breaks in your bio to make it less difficult to go through?

Instagram is rich in features and is suitable for the creation of content that is unique. If you can master some of these relatively unknown features, you will be able to get the best out of Instagram.

Partner with Relevant Influencers

If you are in search of a tried and tested way to give your business the right level of attention, you can explore a partnership with an influencer that is relevant. This will have to be paid for.

It is important to note that influencer partnerships vary in some ways. There are lots of questions that you must provide answers to while trying to get an influencer. Some of these questions are:

- "Do I share the same values, personality, and aesthetic beliefs with the influencer brand I am considering? "

- "Have they partnered with any brand and product which share some features with my brand?"

Make Use of Great Headings

As far as engagement is concerned, captions can be said to be as vital as the videos or images that they augment. With the right caption, you can make your brand's personality known, as well as entertain your audience all at once.

The ideal captions can be read easily, is clear and straight to the point. As a matter of fact, the ideal captions save the reader the time of trying to decipher them. They can be understood effortlessly.

You must know the voice of your brand, as well as your audience if you want to achieve this effect. If you know your audience, you can always have content that interests them. Also, knowing your brand voice will help with consistency.

Make it a practice to try out some copywriting tactics (e.g., ensure that words that are considered most important make it to a caption's beginning). It is equally important to practice these techniques.

Choose Hashtags Wisely

If you are looking to get attention, hashtags cannot be overemphasized. When correctly made use of, a hashtag can direct lots of visitors to your brand, posts, and profile. However, a misleading hashtag, especially when irrelevant or used excessively can bring about lots of negative results.

The reason for this is if a user comes across anything they do not like after following a hashtag, they can always click on the option "Don't Show for This Hashtag".

According to Michael Aynsley, Hootsuite editor, this feature was created to tell the Instagram algorithm the kind of content a specific user like. However, if Instagram flags too many of your posts, it is assumed that your content will come up less or not at all. When making hashtags, you need to consider the following:

- Stay relevant, do not try to stuff hashtags

- Stay specific, have a target audience.

- Do not mistake the meaning of the hashtag for something else

- You must be concise - when a hashtag is short, it is easily remembered.

Get on The Explore Tab

If you want to build the visibility of your brand in the shortest time possible, make use of the Explore tab. With the Explore tab, users can locate content that is curated as a result of the actions that they took in the past. The implication of this is that Instagram is aware of your activities. It is, therefore, able to push related content to you explore tab.

Also, Instagram gets content from accounts which have something in common with those you follow. It is all dependent on pattern recognition and data, and it leads to the question: what are the ways to get your content onto the explore tab? Although there are no specific methods, a lot can be done to give yourself a good chance:

Know Your Audience

Who is your target audience? What are their interests? Who is the people they currently follow on Instagram? To discover what drives engagement with your audience, make use of reverse engineering.

Make Use of Hashtags

One straightforward way to get people to discover your content is to make use of hashtags. When you use hashtags, it makes it easy for your content to be discovered. This is one reason all marketers should make use of them

Encourage Engagement

As the likes, comments, and shares of an Instagram post increases, the likelihood of these posts appearing on the explore tab of your target audience increases.

To get better engagement, you should geo-tag your posts and mention other accounts that are relevant while writing your caption. As the relevance of your post increases, there will be an increase in the likelihood of you compelling more action from your audience.

Target the Right Audience with Ads

Do you find yourself in a space that is very competitive? You might need to make use of Instagram ads to promote your brand.

There are five formats for ads on Instagram: photos, videos, canvas story ads, story ads, and carousels. The feeds or story of your target audience has each format incorporated into it. This, therefore, makes it difficult to omit.

Although it is possible to build your Instagram presence without spending money, you can be confident that it will take a long while. If you want to get things done faster, you should take advantage of ads.

How to Use Instagram Stories for Business?

Making use of Instagram stories to carry out business transactions is currently an essential part of all marketing strategies on Instagram. Doing this can aid you in interacting with customers, and in pushing engagement.

It is not very easy to find ideas for Instagram stories and decide on what you will post. Well, if you require inspiration, below are ways in which businesses make use of Instagram stories.

Promote Your Products And/or Services

Instagram stories have an organic tapping progression. This makes it an excellent place to grow expectations around fresh products.

To do this, simply ensure that your story is packed with various photos of one product at all possible angles, in various environments, and with various people. Once done put a promo code. Once you have enough followers, you'll be able to add clickable links to your Instagram stories.

Build A More Engaged Community

Just like regular posts, when you make use of Instagram stories to promote a business, make it a combination of promotional, light-hearted, and fun content. Instagram stories is not a very serious environment. This, therefore, makes it a good place for every type of post.

Run an Instagram Stories Takeover

A very simple way to make use of Instagram stories is to get an individual to present your story or get involved in an Instagram stories takeover.

With a frequent guest segment, you can spice up your use of Instagram stories. If you want to give it a try with your business, feel free to select anyone from your firm to carry out an everyday life story. You can also swap stories with other businesses in your sector.

Track Your Performance with Instagram Analytics

One straightforward way to stay on course while looking to achieve your marketing targets for Instagram is understanding and tracking your analytics.

Irrespective of what you are trying to track - reach or general engagement, there are ways to get it done quickly. With a business profile, it is easy to access Instagram Insights. Making use of Instagram Insights can help you get all the information you need from a dashboard

Chapter 9:
Abide by these Social Media Marketing Laws

The introduction of social media marketing into the digital industry about a decade ago has brought about significant changes in the marketing process. This has made marketing a lot easier and helps one reach a broader audience within a short period with less stress involved.

If you don't yet understand what social media marketing all is about, the best way to begin is to get acquainted with the basic rules and play by them.

Do you want to grow your business or brand, reach a larger targeted audience and turn them into potential customers? If yes, then here are ten fundamental laws of social media marketing every social media marketer must know and abide by to achieve their desired result.

The Law of Prioritizing Quality
This law encourages you to pay more attention to those followers of yours who show more interest in what you have to offer than those who care less. Rather than trying to build a broader audience of

uninterested followers, create quality content and provide quality products that will keep your active followers interested in your brand or business. Always keep in mind that quality supersedes quantity.

Never underestimate the power of a well-written article. You would rather have one carefully written article than a thousand shabby ones. Do not rush when creating your content, give it the attention and effort it requires and never hesitate to ask for external help if need be.

The Law of Empathetic Listening
If you want to have a stronger impact on your audience, learn to interact with them. Find out which trending topics or subjects' matter to them and include those in your content. By doing this, you keep your followers engaged and active on your page and give them reasons to continually come back for more. It is important that you pay attention to the preferences of your audience and give them what they want. Interact with them in the best way you can, and you are good to go.

The Law of One-Point Focus
Be specific in the products or the services you provide, avoid handling too many different things at the same time. This will limit your efficiency and reduce the quality of your content as you are stretched amongst different things, and finally scare away your customers because you come across to them as confused and unserious.

Choosing a specific niche to operate in gives you a better chance at succeeding than venturing into different unrelated niches. Your area of specialization will determine your customers; it is, therefore, your duty to choose carefully. When the need to look for external aid arises, do not give it a second thought. Always offer your customers and other potential customers the best.

The Law of Adding Value to Voice

The importance of promoting your brand or business can never be overemphasized. However, it is necessary to pay attention to other essential things that will help your brand grow. Ensure the quality of your products and services do not depreciate while you are putting in so much effort at promoting your brand. Post entertaining content occasionally that will excite your audience. Appreciate your customers by giving them incentives such as giveaways, discounts on your products and services, and more. This will go a long way at increasing their loyalty and even attract more potential customers.

Continuous promotion of your products or services without giving your audience something new to chew on might eventually leave them uninterested in your content causing you a massive setback.

The Law of Reciprocated Efforts

This is another law every social media marketer must apply for a better outcome. When a brand or an online influencer with a large followership shares your content on their platform, it is necessary that you reciprocate the favor. Reciprocating widens your reach and promotes your page even more. Therefore, if you wish for your content to be shared by brands and influencers with a large audience, you must also be willing to do the same. Never assume that a big brand or influencer does not need your promotion, it would be selfish of you to expect them to continually share your content without reciprocating. This could cause them to lose interest in your business and focus on those who understand the principle of reciprocation. With the high rate of competition in the world today, applying this law will help you stand out amongst so many similar brands. Your inability to play by this law might cause your business to suffer setbacks or slow your progress.

The Law of Patience

Succeeding at social media marketing requires excellent patience and doesn't happen by chance. To excel at this, you must be willing to put in great effort and time to get the best result. The world is now highly competitive, and mediocrity can barely survive. This is even more reason why you must take your time at creating quality content that will speak to your audience.

Think of social media marketing as an upcoming examination, and your grades depend on the amount of effort you put into your studies. Mere opening of your books and staring at them cannot give you the good grades you desire. This is also applicable to social media marketing as you can only excel when you give it your best and do not quit after a short while.

A lot of businesses throw in the towel and walk away shortly after they venture into social media marketing due to slow progression, forgetting that this process takes time to produce positive results.

The Law of Compounding

This law is the most important of them all. Quality content has a way of reaching out to a broader audience. This is because people value quality more than quantity and do not hesitate to share when they come across it. Therefore, it is essential to give it your best when creating content.

A subscriber who appreciates the quality of your products or services on YouTube might be prompted to tweet about it on Twitter or make a post on Facebook and Instagram encouraging others to visit your channel without being paid to do so. As a result, you may experience an increase in the number of subscribers and views on your post which will eventually translate into financial success.

The Law of Influence

According to this law, it is essential to have a good relationship with brands and online influencers who have many active followers and customers. If they find your content compelling enough, they might decide to share it with their followers exposing you to a broader audience of potential customers.

TIP: Choose the influencers you would like to work with and promote them on your platform. This will enable you to connect with their audience, creating a type of bond between you two. Note that there is always a unique audience for the products and services you offer; however, you must figure out a way to get across to them.

The Law of Acknowledging Everyone

Keep pride and arrogance far away from you. Never ignore a person who reaches out to you. Treat this with the utmost importance and show respect to whoever is involved no matter how occupied you are.

Endeavor to appreciate any post a person makes about you or if you are tagged in a positive post. Merely saying "thank you" or responding politely will give your followers a sense of importance, making them loyal fans. This is a fundamental law you must play by as nobody likes to be ignored.

Your approach towards your social media relationship should be like that of a physical one. People will stay loyal to you when you appreciate their efforts towards your growth. Instead of treating them as a mere pawn that is of little value, show them love and let them know how much you value their effort.

The Law of Accessibility

Keeping your audience engaged is always of great importance. Do not make the mistake of continually ignoring your audience or not interacting with them. This will kill your brand faster than you can imagine. When you publish a post, stay on it and respond to comments and questions as much as you can. Social media is a two-way street, and communication is key to growth. It is much easier to forget businesses or brands that are not easily accessible.

To avoid stagnancy or decline in the growth of your business, prove to your audience that you are readily available for them. Let your actions speak for you. Do your best to reply to every direct message sent to your brand page inbox within 24 hours as it is rude and unprofessional to ignore them. Always be available to respond to the needs of your customers.

Although a lot of businesses are aware of the benefit of social media marketing, only a few have a deep understanding of how it works and take advantage of it.

Never forget that to succeed at social media marketing you must consistently create posts and offer products and services that appeal to the desires of your clients. However, to achieve this, it is essential to apply the right approach. Design effective strategies that will help you reach your desired audience and never hesitate to make amends or request for external help when the need arises.

Chapter 10:
Convert Followers to Customers

Now that you have a decent number of fans and followers on your social media page, and have followed all the provided steps, you're probably wondering, "How do I convert these followers into actual customers?"

This is a question lots of businesses on social media tend to ask themselves later.

It does not have to be complicated if you know what to do. Below are a few tips that will make this process seamless and provide you with the customer base you require.

Analyze Every Social Channel

If you want to convert followers and fans into customers and make connections, you need to know which social media platform supports your efforts the most.

Start by analyzing the available information you have for every social media channel. Some questions you need to figure out include:

- Which of your social media platforms has the largest audience?

- Which of them has had the most success in keeping your audience engaged?

- Which of them has helped in generating the most business leads?

- What are your followers saying regarding your business on social media?

- What are your followers saying on social media generally, and how can you integrate this into your business?

While analyzing your social profiles is crucial, it is also important to keep an eye on your niche and industry. What are the significant conversations taking place and how do they identify with your business strategy?

To go further and inform the decisions you make, you can utilize data from Twitter, Facebook, and Google Analytics.

Using this data, you can place focus on the most important social media websites, then adjust your content strategy before creating posts that complement that strategy.

Understand Your Target Audience

If you want to be successful in social media marketing, you need to point out your target market clearly. Carry out research and create a customer persona that will aid you in this. What age range does your target market include?

Let us assume you have pointed out your target market, and they are in the age groups of 17 – 25. You have a Facebook page, which is ideal because over 80 percent of that audience has a profile on Facebook.

But you are not efficiently making use of your profiles if you are not using Snapchat, YouTube, and Instagram.

While it is crucial to be on as many channels as possible, your target audience will determine the level of input you require on each one. For those who are only marketing to individuals over the age of 50, it is not effective focusing your marketing efforts on Tumblr and Snapchat.

But a few of your businesses may have a broader range of services and products which converts into a more diverse target market. You will have to utilize every social channel in a different manner, based on the users you want to reach.

If you are trying to sell glasses to a 60 year old, Snapchat will not be the channel for this. Ensure your promotions are relevant for the social channel you are utilizing.

Concentrate Your Social Media Efforts

Now that you are aware of which social media platform has the most importance to your business, and you have a clear definition of your audience, you need to concentrate your efforts.

Except you have a social media team managing your social media, you will need to put in a lot of effort yourself. There is no benefit to your business if you have a presence on five websites and ignore them all until, they die off.

It is best to concentrate on 1 or 2 websites and work with those. Once you are successful, you can move onto other sites. You can also use your audience metrics to aid you in pinpointing the social media channel you want to head to.

Let's presume you are doing well on Facebook and one of your targets is 60 years old; you will want to consider a channel more popular and significant to individuals around 60 years and above. It is also crucial that irrespective of the social media platform you are using, that you offer quality content that urges them to head to your website. If your content is very engaging, your level of success is going to be high.

For example, let us assume you are in the food niche. Develop an exciting and relevant blog post on the best Japanese meals. Add a link to a significant landing page on your site. Ensure the link is related to the content and not just any page on the website.

You can also use the blog post as a means of getting clients to sign up to your email list. The more often you keep in touch with clients, the more likely they will consider your business when they have the need for a product or service you sell.

Have A Thorough Understanding of The Chosen Platform

The instant you know the platform that works perfectly for your business, you need to learn how to utilize that platform efficiently. Using the information, you have amassed, you will have the ability to develop a strategy around specific content. However, you will be unable to utilize the same content on all platforms.

Remember, what works on Twitter may not work on Facebook. The same is also applicable to your Instagram and YouTube posts.

Your content needs to have the same focus but with different strategies. Below are a few examples:

- A blog post on LinkedIn on how particular meal ingredients could be harmful to your health which links back to your page of healthy food ingredients you sell.

- A picture of healthy meals with their ingredients on Instagram which links back to the post of healthy food ingredients.

- A Twitter post about your most recent meal using hashtags about trending topics you have researched.

- A link on Facebook to your blog post alongside a call to action to share and like your page.

Promote and Sell

You can also convince fans and followers to buy your products. You can do this using sales exclusives and deals.

For example, post coupons exclusive to your audience on Facebook. It is not difficult to provide coupon codes but are only announcing to fans or followers of your Facebook page.

Customers enjoy feeling special, and Facebook gives you the ability to make them feel so. Discounts exclusive to followers of your page will be more cherished by your clients. This could not only enhance the number of followers you have but also, aid in turning individuals who like your page into buyers.

The promotion does not have to be an immediate purchase or sale for a limited time. There are studies which show that 40 percent of individuals will like a page on Facebook if it means you will provide them with a discount on their subsequent order. Another choice is to send a coupon to blog subscribers in a newsletter. While selling products at a lower price, you will end up with lots more sales as a result of the promotion which could also result in continuous sales.

Think Past Your Organization

To establish a presence that clients will keep coming back to and consider when shopping, it is a good idea to think past your own content.

For example, you can use Facebook to link to posts that will relate to the interests of your audience occasionally, and not only link to your organization's page.

On Twitter, you can post quotes that inspire your audience, or provide questions to your audience using hashtags like "What is the biggest frustration for people when trying to eat healthily?" Twitter is also a means for people to find news, so you can develop tweets using trending pop culture topics or sharing content of influencers that are significant to your organization.

Engaging and fun content will bring you a broader social media presence and will ensure you always remain first in the minds of clients. Consider channeling your effort in developing a presence that goes beyond sales. Some professionals have recommended that you follow an 80/20 rule. You will focus only 20 percent of your posts on sales and content, while the rest should be on more general information your audience would find relevant. Find a middle ground that works for you and your organization.

Do You Have Loyal Fans?
Loyal fans translate into loyal customers. But, for a follower to transform into a loyal follower, you as the owner of the business must show loyalty first.

Frequency and consistency will help show your loyalty. To get this done, post content in a consistent manner. Whether this implies posting on precise days every week, or an exact number of times every day, your followers will begin to look forward to your messages.

It is okay to take a break but be sure you inform your followers about it. For example, if you are going on vacation, tell them and let them know you will miss them and look forward to sharing pictures and content when you come back. You can also let them know that you will be in touch intermittently during your absence. This shows that you respect their loyalty.

Similarly, to show you care, inform them that their thoughts are important to you. When they respond, leave a comment. Prove that you care about them continuously, just the way you do when you interact with your actual friends every day.

Provide Your Followers with Exclusive Deals

Make your customers feel special. Providing your followers with exclusive deals will ensure they come back continuously. These deals do not have to be complicated, instead, keep them fun and simple.

For instance: "20% off all our packages if you purchase today, exclusive to our followers on Twitter. Send us an email and mention you saw this post." You can even begin a deal of the week. This will ensure followers keep checking in and coming back for more.

Be Responsive and Active

When you have attained lots of followers and reached some sales objectives using your presence on social media, you should continue being active and responding to your clients.

One of the most important aspects of social media marketing is to post frequently and keep being relevant to your followers. You can utilize tools to schedule posts and maintain a consistent posting presence. Irrespective of how you achieve it, these frequent updates will leave your name in the minds of your potential clients and existing clients.

Also, you need to respond to your clients. You need to respond to any comments or questions on your website quickly. Any customer or potential client will value an honest and fast response, so ensure you are available to those who reach out to you using social media.

Facebook users expect a speedy reply to their messages. Spending too much time before you respond or failing to respond will hurt your image, and one bad communication can leave lasting adverse effects.

On the bright side, you can also use positive comments and interactions of clients to promote your business further. Spend extra time each day updating and monitoring your presence on social media.

Invite Them to Something Personalized and Entertaining
Offer your followers some VIP attention. For example, invite all your followers on Instagram to a live video feed where you will be responding to their questions in your area of expertise.

Inform them that this is just for your followers on Instagram and you will respond to only a specific number of individuals. You can do something similar on Facebook via your fan page or on Twitter using hashtags. Be sure to inform them that you will be available to provide solutions to their problems.

You can also allow your followers to submit questions in advance through direct messaging, and only those that you receive within a specific time will get a response. This will also ensure your event goes smoothly as you do not have to wait for anyone to join the live feed to ask a question.

Promote Your Audience

This is an excellent method of building credibility, giving back and strengthening your relationships. As soon as you have developed a good relationship with your followers, they will transform into customers.

Choose a day of the week on Instagram to promote one of your followers. This does not imply you should mention five followers and do a photo-mix of them. This is neither promotional nor personal. Instead, choose some followers that you always engage with and mention why you value their input.

On Facebook, there is an application that can help with this. You can include the fan of the week application to your fan page.

Allow Your Clients And Customers to Have A Say

Pay attention to the encouraging things clients and customers say about your products and business. One method of doing this is by asking, perhaps at the end of a coaching call, "What is the most important thing you learned today?" Then also ask, "Can I share your takeaway on Twitter or Facebook?"

Sharing testimonials reminds your followers about the services and products you offer. But, further than that, it proves that others have found your products or services to be useful.

Try Out Paid Ads on Social Media

Spending on social media applications is a fantastic method of developing a targeted following. Almost every core social media channel which includes Instagram, Facebook and LinkedIn, provide paid ads.

You can use these to enhance your content views, reach, engagements and clicks. You can get the best of your investments with offers and reconstruct past posts to target possible clients. In doing this, you will be able to get new subscribers, followers and potential leads for the future.

The best aspect of ads is the ability to get precise with your demographic targeting. You will be able to tailor a variety of ads to various personas with fantastic accuracy. This enhances the possibility of targeting more business clients.

Offer Customer Service on Social Media

Fantastic customer service is often the deciding element that makes customers pick one business over another to purchase from. This is because your efforts are always displayed publicly.

More than 80 percent of customers utilize social media to speak directly to businesses, and it also happens to be their method of preference for customer care. Replying quickly to resolve the queries of your customers can aid in enhancing trust and significantly boost your reputation.

Offering amazing customer support on social media is a fantastic method of enhancing business via word of mouth marketing. What is more, you will be able to develop positive press for yourself, which can have a positive impact on your customer procurement on social media.

Utilizing social media in promoting and marketing your business can take a lot of time, but the rewards are tremendous. Taking time to develop your strategy before you leap can provide you with the results you desire.

Utilize all available data, understand your channel, develop content significant for it and your followers, and ensure that they remain responsive and active.

Don't get discouraged when you reach your first hurdle. Analyze and make changes as required, and social media will be a useful addition to your business strategy.

Chapter 11:
Proven Social Media Secrets

In the digital world today, your availability on social media is of great value to the growth of your business. Your business might experience slow progress if you are nonchalant towards utilizing the power of social media marketing.

Right from the beginning, online communities have been an integral part of the Internet, and social media today has been widely accepted all over the world. As a matter fact, are there are estimated to be about 2.62 billion online social media users, and by 2021 it is expected that this value will rise above 3 billion.

Therefore, social media is the best marketing platform for businesses, even more so for business owners that wish to broaden their reach. Finding and applying proven social media techniques is paramount to achieving this goal.

We shall be looking at a few essential social media tools that will give you an edge in effective marketing and business growth.

There Is No Specific Formula for Successful Marketing

According to Puranjay Singh, although a good number of experts have written books and formulas that are believed to be generally effective in marketing, they are sometimes not effective. Creating and publishing posts as often as possible might work for someone else but not for you. This article might sound very affirmative and compelling to follow; nevertheless, there is no specific written formula for successful online marketing.

The uniqueness of every brand or business depends on the problem they are offering a solution to and the nature of the audience involved. Not to mention that social media is ever changing and so is the character of those involved. This makes it even more difficult to have a generalized approach to building a brand online.

Would your approach towards marketing a florist and an eatery online be the same? Of course not. You must first carry out a careful study of your audience, then figure out the best way to reach out and turn them into customers for each business.

To measure your performance as an online marketer, below are a few tools that can be beneficial to you.

Content curation app, DrumUp provides you with content that improves your engagement. This app helps you save time by creating an account for multiple account management.

Image optimization app PicMonkey, this enables you to do justice to your images. It also has canvases for different purposes and ready-made templates to suit your needs.

With Google Analytics you can monitor your efforts and know which of your social media platforms are most effective for your online marketing.

Social Mention is a social media monitoring tool that helps you monitor things such as competition, important keywords, and brand mentions.

Engaged Following Is A Prerequisite for High ROI

Every social media marketer focus should be on their ROI, except if you aren't looking forward to making any progress. Building a followership is always a challenge in the initial stages. This is because it takes time and quality content to attract your audience and make them stick around unlike TV and radio station marketing that doesn't require as much effort.

Irrespective of the quality of your content at the beginning, you might still record a low rate of engagement. But applying the right approach and consistently publishing quality content will enable you to achieve that ROI you desire.

Creating A Specific Marketing Strategy Is Important

Research has shown that a large number of marketer's lack strategies to reach their target audience. To build an audience of active followers, creating a marketing strategy is paramount. What is effective content?

- Content that brings about the desired response from an audience

- Content that is relevant to an audience

- Content with an engaging storyline

Challenges Marketers Face with Content Creation

- Inability to monitor the progress of your efforts - to overcome this get a social media monitoring app

- The difficulty in creating content that will captive and engage the targeted audience.

- Limited time to create quality content - this can be dealt with using content curation apps.

- Difficulty in matching content and required volume.

It is crucial to document your strategy as it helps you stay focused and confident in your actions.

Publicity Can Come in Different Ways

Just like in the physical world, people promote their businesses and brands through the referral method of "tell someone to tell someone" which could be done by customers, fans, employees or business partners. This can also be applied to social media marketing. Building a good relationship with your online customers will encourage them to promote your brand by introducing your business to their friends and family. Positive feeds and testimonies from your customers are also beneficial.

You can also pay online influencers with a large following to promote your product and services on their platform for a specific period.

You could also partner with other businesses and strike a deal with them. This may require you to promote each other's products and services on your respective platforms. You could also leverage your employees into promoting the business and show your appreciation with incentives.

Ability to Understand the Significance of Data Is Crucial.
Until you can understand the information behind your data and capitalize on it for improvement, limitations will keep locking up your business. This is to say that data interpretation is of great necessity in the process of marketing.

Data itself is limited in action and depends on you for specific clarification. No algorithm can detect the impression people have about your business. Therefore, it is your sole responsibility to have a proper understanding of the data your content generates.

It'll be disastrous for your brand if you build your strategy around data alone. Utilizing the information from your data and applying other formulas to create an effective strategy should be non-negotiable.

As observed, businesses tend to grow faster on social media when there is an interaction between the audience and the marketer. Never neglect your audience if you desire continuous growth.

Focus also on your connection with people outside of social media. Your ability to maintain cordial relationships with your clients should be of the utmost importance.

Strange Social Media Tips That Work

Above, we have covered some proven social media secrets. Now, let us take a look at some strange tips that can help your brand.

Stir Controversy

Marketers who know what they are doing utilize controversy as a means of driving social engagement and traffic. Including the element of controversy in your social media campaigns aids in the following:

- Creating a buzz about your brand or organization

- Pushes massive traffic to your profiles on social media

- Enhances your engagement metrics and follower base

So, how do you develop controversy? Below are a few of the best methods:

Take a different view regarding generally accepted information or facts. For example, if everyone detests a vehicle model, you can gain attention by going the opposite route.

Talk about a taboo subject in your field. For example, if you are into dog training, then speak about using electric collars for dog training.

Pick on Trending Hashtags

As you must be aware, Hashtags aid in classifying or grouping posts on social media. For example, #NewYear.

Additionally, trending hashtags are those trending on a specific day or time. For example: On 25th December each year, #Christmas is a trending hashtag.

This strategy needs you to utilize trending hashtags on your posts to amass peak exposure. But, how do you find a trending hashtags list? There are lots of tools like Trendsmap that can help you out with that. However, in using Hashtags, you need to be careful of the following:

Don't Use Excess Hashtags. Except if an individual has lots of patience, he or she won't go through a lengthy list of hashtags. Place the most significant ones at the start and the most entertaining ones at the end. These are two locations individuals have a high likelihood of reading.

Don't Develop Long Hashtags: Since it is more difficult to read without spaces, restrict them to four words

Don't Utilize Hashtags That Beg for Followers. Having lots of followers is great but having real and engaged individuals is better. Begging for people to follow you is not professional. Stay away from hashtags like #like4like or anything that others would see as pandering.

Don't Forget to Read Through. If you leave spaces out of some words, they will read differently.

Tag an Influencer
An influencer is a personality on social media who has lots of impact on his or her followers. Influencers create relevant content, curate and share the content of others. Aside from that, they are also an excellent source of industry information and news.

Generally, followers act based on the opinions and advice of influencers. They influence their followers' decisions.

But, how exactly can influencers aid you in achieving your social media marketing objectives? It is easy. Say, for example, you wrote a post about freelance writing and tagged a recognized personality on social media. If the influencer you tagged likes your post and retweets or shares it with his followers, your post would instantly be exposed to lots of people.

Make Use of Emojis

Social media is a place filled with lots of businesses trying to grab as many viewers as possible. So, how do you ensure your brand is heard? Why not try emojis?

Emojis tend to capture the eyes of viewers because they are appealing. Additionally, they also make your posts seem more genuine.

Observe Your Competitors

Copying everything your competitor does is not good for business. But checking out other accounts can get your creative juices going.

Find out these facts about your competitors and other leading social media brands. What hashtags are they using? What types of posts are garnering lots of shares or comments?

You can also look at those who have the most interaction with your competitors and follow them. If they are taking time to interact with your competitor, there is a huge possibility that they will also engage with you as well.

Aside from this, you could also try liking or following the posts of your competitors. Just because they are your competitors, it does not mean you can't be friends.

Chapter 12:
Double Down on Social Media Marketing NOW

The benefits of Social Media Marketing cannot be overemphasized. Now is the time to take advantage of this wonderful strategy if you want to grow your business. At present, social media marketing is one of the cheapest means of reaching your customers. It is a resource that a lot of companies are not taking advantage of yet. But it can have a massive impact on your marketing if you do it correctly.

You need to double down on social media marketing now because it won't always remain as cheap as it is. Over time, the cost is likely going to rise, and it will be more difficult for you as a brand to corner the market as opposed to right now. That is not all. All your clients and potential clients are on social media right now which is why you need to take advantage and reach them soon.

Twitter, Instagram and Facebook are great platforms which will help you go from unknown to widely known. You need to take advantage of these platforms.

Above, I have provided you with many strategies that you can read and implement to make your brand a social media juggernaut. Now, all that is left is for you to invest and use these strategies to draw in loyal subscribers.

If you know you are not taking advantage of social media, then these strategies will certainly be of help. By the time you complete this book, you will have a comprehensive understanding of why social media marketing is important and why you should channel more of your marketing efforts into it.

So why wait? Take that step today and watch yourself become the next social media millionaire.

Social Media Marketing Plan How To

Build A Magnetic Brand Making You A Known Influencer. Go from Zero to One Million Followers In 30 Days. Apply The 1-Page Advertising Secret to Stand Out

Chapter 1:
What Is A Brand

The Brand

A brand is what makes a person or business stand out from others. It is the way the target audience perceives a product, service, or experience due to its design, logo, name, and slogans.

The Business

A business is an organization which tries to satisfy the needs of various individuals to gain profits by selling products and services that solve the problem of the audience.

What Differentiates A Brand from A Business?

A business focuses more on how to generate profits by offering products and services to its target audience. The brand, on the other hand, is a culmination of the experience that members of the target audience will have any time they interact with the business.

Elements of A Brand

Various elements make a brand. Understanding these elements is a more straightforward way to understand a brand better. These include brand identity, compass, personality, voice, and more.

Brand Compass

The basic facts about a brand are summarized within the brand compass. It includes the strategic objectives, mission, purpose, values, and vision of a brand. The brand compass is the result of the research, positioning, and brand strategy.

Brand Personality

The emotional and behavioral qualities of a brand form the brand personality. These are traits which closely relate with the brand. Through the brand personality, it is possible to connect with the target audience. A brand identity makes a brand easy to identify by individuals loyal to the brand. There are some aspects of a brand which also form the brand personality. These include the brand logo, its design, tagline, and more.

Brand Name and Tagline

The brand name is one of the easiest ways through which your audience can interact with the brand. It also applies to the tagline. Coming up with a tagline and a brand name requires testing, brainstorming, market research, and refinement. Through these processes, the brand name and slogan will be unique and meaningful. The values of a brand are usually identifiable from the name and tagline. It also differentiates a brand from its competition.

Brand Image

A brand image is merely the expectations that the target audience has a brand. It through the brand image that the target audience can predict the next step a brand will take. Through the brand image Apple has developed, none of their customers will be expecting an iPhone with running on the Android operating system. Also, it is also possible to predict that the net iPhone will run on iOS with improvements to the features which the phone offers. It is a clear indication of the brand image which the company has developed.

Brand Identity

There are a few things which are present in a brand strategy. These will include the promise, purpose, and personality of a brand. The brand identity is a visual representation of all these aspects. It is the real meaning behind the brand logo. As a visual, it should be able to communicate the core ideas of the brand to anyone who sees it. It is also straightforward to promote easy identification. Combining the logo with a tagline is a method which creates a brand identity that is recognizable worldwide.

Brand Voice and Messaging

The brand voice and its messaging determine how the brand will engage with its audience. These two elements are essential in delivering the personality, purpose, and promise of a brand. It also instills humanity in the brand. The brand voice should be easily recognizable by your audience. It doesn't matter the channel through which the message is coming.

Brand Website

The brand website is where your brand delivers content to engage with its audience. Using smartphones, your audience can access the brand website on the go and in any location. Providing a high-quality brand experience is more cost-effective through the brand website.

Brand Equity

The value of a brand is what I refer to as brand equity. It includes both the tangible and intangible aspects such as revenue, strategic benefits, and market shares.

Brand Gap

The disparity between what a brand can do and the promises the brand makes form the brand gap. For a brand to be successful, it needs a low brand gap. It implies that the brand should be able to deliver on the promises it makes to its customers. Promising a superior quality product at a low price and delivering an inferior quality product at a low price will cause a considerable brand gap.

Why Invest in Branding?

The perception of a business often determines if it will invest in a brand or not. The main reason for this difference in perception is the inability to relate a brand to the increase in returns directly. In truth, there is no way to evaluate the value of a brand. It is why a lot of businesses hesitate. If you cannot assess the value, why do you need to build a brand? A lot of businesses consider a brand to be an investment. As such, it is just an additional expense. Realizing that a brand is the only way to influence the behavior of the target customer will change this belief. Incorporating a brand into the long-term strategy of the business will yield profits all through the life of the company. Here are some of the benefits of a brand:

Branding Improves Recognition

An essential element of a brand is the brand logo. The logo serves as the face of the business. It is the first thing your audience will recollect about your brand. To design a logo, having a professional design is your best bet. The logo needs to be simple and easy to remember. A logo should reflect your ideal company image to your audience. If your company is within a niche in the gaming industry, having a gamepad on a stack of books can be misleading to your audience. Your target audience needs to be able to tell what your company does by a simple look at its logo.

Branding Creates Trust

By creating a brand, it is possible to develop trust between the company and its customers. A great brand will also provide the look of an industry expert. The target audience is usually willing to interact with a brand since it offers a professional outlook. It is noticeable in the way it provides its services and performs its operations.

Branding Promotes Marketing

A brand is the most effective form of marketing a business can invest in. If a brand is recognized, it becomes easier for marketing to achieve its goals. Since developing a brand will require a lot of market research, it is possible to use this market research to reach the target audience.

Branding Builds Financial Value

Building a strong brand usually increases the value of a business. It is the main reason why a company will have valuable stocks. The stocks don't indicate the actual value of the assets but the value of the brand. A company that grows its brand properly will reap its benefits during IPO sales or when it needs to source for funds. In addition to the increase in share prices, your customers will also be able to justify the rise in the prices of products. It becomes the ideal definition of customers buying a brand. An established brand name makes it easy to attract premium prices. The increase in value through a brand also makes it profitable for a business owner any time the need to sell the business arises.

Motivation to You and Your Employees

The brand is something that you are working towards. It is essential to have something to work towards to serve as a goal. That is what your brand is to your employees. A strong brand will cause employees to feel a sense of pride when working. The brand is something the entire team can rally around.

Branding Generates New Customers

Having a strong brand develops customer loyalty. Word-of-mouth marketing is one of the benefits of having loyal customers. It is also well-known that customer loyalty is an essential factor in business. Since your loyal customers will be assisting in the marketing of your brand, you are more likely to attract your ideal customers. These are customers who will also be willing to buy into your brand and remain loyal to the brand.

It Allows You Charge A Premium Price

According to the old saying, people buy brands and not products. For these reasons, individuals don't mind paying premium prices for premium brands. Branding offers you the chance to place yourself as a leader in the industry with a persuasive set of values none of your competitors offer. Brands that make themselves unique can validate their worth and charge higher than their competitors for their services and products. As we are all aware, increase in price means an increase in revenue.

Close Sales with More Ease

The difference between trying to sell a brand that outdated and boring, and one that is fresh and unique is like the difference between our former landlines and the new android phone. It is easier to sell a properly defined brand because they have established their position in the narrative of their brand. The arguments as to how your brand as unique and superior services or products has already being portrayed through the strategy of your brand. With a compelling and cohesive brand, most of the salesperson's work has already been done before the first conversation. Branding offers your sales team the upper hand it requires to swiftly, easily and confidently close deals.

Minimize Cost of Marketing

A brand which is well-articulated and cohesive enhances the effectiveness and efficiency of your marketing initiatives. By understanding your audience better alongside customer interviews, you will be able to create campaigns with a very significant message which targets your most relevant customer groups. You won't have to waste any more efforts on blind messaging. Brand cohesiveness also implies that any effort you make is incorporated with ease as all your initiatives aid in reinforcing one another. Your bold identity also implies that you differentiate your campaigns right from the start. Lastly, the templates and guidelines that come up from the process of branding make certain that you do not have to revamp the wheel on design each time you want to create another marketing initiative.

Tips to Take Control of Your Business Brand Identity

Establish your visual identity which goes with your projects and vision, or the target audience your organization wishes to work with

Pay attention to your reputation online, so you don't get surprised. Ask satisfied clients to offer you great reviews on Google or other review sites which help in catering to your market niche

Provide the experience your customers expect from all interaction that takes place from phone conversations, customer service, websites and sent emails. Treat your clients the way you would want a company to treat you if you were a client

Broaden your visibility on social networks and your community. Developing relationships are essential to building a brand, and the best method of doing it is to aid individuals in ways that make you stand out.

Do not forget that if you own a business, you have a brand. It is up to you to decide what to do with it and determine how others perceive you. If your brand goes with your visions and places emphasis on the requirements of your target audience, it can aid in attracting the appropriate customers to your organization.

Brand Evaluation

It is any meaningful and relevant feedback regarding the brand. Is the brand reaching its target audience? The feedback should come from the target audience for it to be relevant. If the feedback on a brand is coming from family and friends, it may not mirror the actual problems of the brand. There are specific indications that a brand is not doing too well.

"What Is A Brand?"

This is a problem that is common to a lot of businesses. Many businesses do not recognize a brand or its importance. Some businesses may also neglect the brand for a few years. It doesn't matter how important the business is to you as an entrepreneur; the brand is also a part of the business. Creating a brand platform makes it easy for your team to begin building.

There Is Nothing Unique About the Brand

No brand is built as an exact copy of a more successful brand. Nonetheless, there are often subtle similarities between certain brands. When evaluating the uniqueness of a brand, it is essential to ask a few questions. Questions like how often do competitors think up an event like what you had in mind? Are my competitors usually making comments like what you will make as a brand? These can be simple pointers to a lack of uniqueness in your brand. If you can state multiple areas where your brand differs from the competition, then this is not an issue. A competitor continually coming up with your ideas signifies the need for re-evaluation.

People Misunderstand the Brand

The goal of a brand is to connect with its target audience. It is evident that the target audience should have a clear understanding of what the brand offers. If there is a clear understanding of a brand by its target audience, other audiences should also be able to understand that it is not their ideal brand. It is crucial since you don't want to build a following or email list full of people who are irrelevant to the brand. It will usually lead to a waste of resources. The wrong audience will also misunderstand the brand message making it meaningless. Can people easily recollect what the brand does? Is it easy to describe?

Drop-In Conversions

A drop-in conversion rates over a period is an issue you need to look out for. As soon as a brand notices this trend, it is time to identify the cause. It could be an issue with the perception of the brand. Changes in this perception may also be a cause. It could also indicate a problem with the marketing strategy of the brand. It is a clear case of a branding strategy that doesn't effectively communicate the brand to the target audience. The numbers will only show that there is a problem. It is only through brand evaluation that the brand can identify the problem.

Chapter 2:
Social Media and Personal Branding

A lot of people have defined social media as applications that have been installed on their phones or tablets, but the plain fact is that social media started as a tool used for communication on computers. Social media can be defined as websites and application that are initially designed for people to have easy access to information which they could also in turn share efficiently to one another within a given period. The misconception that social media is an app that is meant for phones, smartphones to be precise, arise from the fact that most users of social media make use of apps to have access to the various tools that they want to make use of.

In truth, the ability to have easy access to photos, events, opinions of others and other information generally within a short period has done a lot of good. It has helped to change the way people live their lives, and it has also contributed one way or the other to improve the businesses of people, the way to run their business to be precise. Retail traders that engage the services of social media as an essential part of their marketing strategy always get impressive results. We also know that the best way to successfully engage social media is to treat it equally without any extra attachment as the other forms of marketing are also addressed.

The History of Social Media

The development of social media started many years ago, evidence of which is seen in some sites of today such as Facebook. The roots of social media are quite deeper than anybody can ever imagine.

Before The 1900s

Letters were the earliest means of communication. It is a means that was used to communicate across long distances, and it is delivered through passing from one hand to the other. Postal services were developed as far back as 550 B.C. Though it may be considered primitive, this delivery system is on the verge of spreading wide even in centuries to come.

Another means of communication known as telegraph was introduced in the year 1792. This medium enabled the delivery of long-distance messages. It is a medium that is so fast that it was quicker than sending a horse rider to deliver. The only thing about this form of communication is that the information it could carry is usually short. The method was anyway a new revolutionary means for sending messages or information across to people. The technique is no longer common outside the banking sector, but it still made delivery of letters easy in the year 1855 through a pneumatic post. It transported capsules from one location to the other using pressurized air tubes.

The telephone was created in the year 1890 and a year later, which is 1891, radio signals were also produced. In the 1800s, there were two significant discoveries in the last decade. Though modernized versions have taken over their predecessors, these forms of technology are still in use. These methods, telephone line, and radio signals have helped people over the years to communicate at high speed to people in faraway places at a given time. These inventions are like a new experience for the whole of humanity.

Development of Social Media in the 20th Century

In the 20th century, technology took a new turn as changes were occurring rapidly. The invention of the first ever supercomputers was in the 1940s, and after that, engineers and scientists began to brainstorm on different ways to connect these computers in such a way that network is created between them. This new development led to the discovery of the Internet. The development of the early versions of the internet like CompuServe started in the 1960s. Baby steps were also taken towards emailing at this period. As at the 70s, there had been significant improvements in networking technology, and virtual newsletters were available as a means of communication among users of UseNet. It was created in 1979.

In the 1980s, the transition of computers into household items had begun as home computers were being installed in homes. Social media was also becoming more stylish. In 1988, IRCs were used for the first time, and its popularity grew well into the 1990s. Six degrees was the first social media site to be recognized, and it was created in 1979. Users had the opportunity to create a profile and meet friends on Six Degrees. The original blogs also became popular in the year 1999, and it did a job of creating a social media stir that is still popular until today.

The Present Day

The popularity of social media began to grow immensely with the aid of the invention of blogging sites. Sites such as Myspace and LinkedIn became prominent sites in the early 2000s, sites such as photo bucket and Flicker aided online photo sharing. The creation of YouTube in 2005 gave people a new experience. A unique experience that enabled people to communicate and share the news in both far and near places. Facebook and Twitter also became available to people for use all over the world, and these sites still retain their status on the internet as the most popular sites. Some other sites such as Tumblr, Spotify, Foursquare and Pinterest were also created to fill up specific spaces in social networking.

In recent times, so many social networking sites have been created such that they are now interlinked to one another. The result of this is that users can now reach as many people as possible or even as many as they want without having to breach the one-to-one relationship they are privileged within communication. The future of social media in decades and even centuries to come is quite not clear as speculations can only be made. The only clear fact about it is that it will always exist in one way or the other if human living is concerned.

Your Personal Branding

Your personal branding has to do with the way you package yourself. It is the combination of the unique way you do the things that you want the world to see about you, a combination of your skills, experience, personality such that it tells your story, portrays the way you comport yourself, shows your behavior, spoken words, written words, and attitudes. Your personal branding is what people use to judge your professional state. Your personal brand could be a combination of how people look at you in real life, the kind of things the media says about you, the type of impression that forms in people's mind from the information they can get about you from social media.

You can choose to ignore your personal brand to enable it to grow naturally. By this, your personal brand tends to be disorganized and beyond your control. You can also choose to form your personal brand into what it is that you want it to be. Before the invention of the Internet, your business card was the only personal brand you have. The only people who were heard of by everyone or most people were those that have high profiles in the media, those who are referred to as hot cakes, also those who appeared as the face of advertisements. But in the world of today where there is no discreteness in social media; every piece of information is spilled, and there is a lower tendency for anonymity.

Why You Would Want A Personal Brand

Your personal brand can be a significant factor. It can be of crucial importance to your profession. It has to do with your presentation before potential and already made clients. It enables you to ensure that you are presented to people in the exact form which you want not in some other and probably detrimental way. It helps you to be able to know your strengths, your weaknesses, and your passions as well. It presents a kind of make-believe image that makes people believe they know you more than they do. It helps people to have a higher trust in you because they feel they know you; this applies to even public figures which they have never met personally. Clear evidence of this is noticeable during the period of election. A lot of people do not take their time to do their findings on the views of the candidates on issues that matter to them; they go directly for a recognized person. It should not come as a surprise that candidates with strong personalities irrespective of their political orientation succeed in politics. It cannot be argued for instance that Donald Trump has built a strong personal brand that helped a lot of people trustingly cast their votes in his favor.

The Importance of Social Media in Personal Branding

To be influential in today's world, you need to create a solid personal brand. Having a personal brand is important because it makes you different from every other person in your field. Your personal brand can help you show off your knowledge and skills in that area. It gives people something to remember you for and separates you from the multitudes surrounding you.

Modern people dislike advertising on a general level; neither do they trust the brands that make them. However, they like and trust people that they feel they know. This observation has influenced how businesses think to market themselves and has led to the popularity and general success of influence marketing today.

Personalizing the main people in a business is now a trend. But while this is easy for small businesses run by sole proprietors, it is difficult for larger companies. Some of them have mastered it well though.

It is logical that before trying to sell a company's message, the owner or manager should first establish a relationship with the potential market. Observe the following on how social media improves personal branding:

Social Media Helps You Announce to The World What You Have to Offer

By function and features, you should note that social media helps you spread the word out about your business. As a result, by not being actively involved in social media, you are significantly limiting your business' chance of getting a good exposure.

Through social media, you can gain brand recognition, develop the brand, and build a likeness for it. On social media, you can create a loyal customer or fan base. More importantly, you can develop your relationship with your target market.

People you engage with on social media including followers and fans will do business with you and refer their friends within and outside social media to you for future business.

Social Media Helps to Enhance Your Search Engine Visibility

Search engine optimization (SEO) works in increasing visibility of contents in search engine results. Many factors influence the search engine ranking of your website and having a social media presence is one of them. Other important factors include mobile optimization of your site, page load speed, linking relationships, and web content. You will have more visibility due to a higher rank in the search engine. Rankings of 95% and usually land on the first page of the search result.

You can maintain a constant social media presence when you always post good content that resonates with your audience. Doing this will have a positive impact on your search results and create more linking relationships. In short, you can't ignore social media if you want high visibility for your business.

Social Media Helps You See into The World of Potential Customers

In every business and every industry, knowing about your potential market is a big priority. Without knowing your audience and understanding what resonates with them, you can't create and deliver the kind of content that they need to see to be willing to patronize your business.

You have the option of conducting research through focus groups and administering surveys, but these can be costly, frivolous, and ineffective in the long run because they can't be done frequently enough.

On the other hand, you can take advantage of social media which encourages interaction on mutual grounds and exchange of information. You get to learn more about your market while they can also explore your social media pages to learn more about you.

No doubt, when used properly, social media is a cheap, fast, and effective way to get information about your audience. You can use that information to grow your business.

Social Media Can Increase Your Web Traffic

Social media is an excellent way for you to be found online and another avenue to invite people to your website. Your every activity on social media is a potential way to lead people to your business website. Therefore, the more you engage your social media pages and your followers, the higher the chances you have at bringing traffic to patronize your site.

The way this works is that your social media will raise curiosity about and your business and in trying to find out more, your audience will do find their way into your website. Social media gives a good return on engagement and will be worth the time you invest in it towards your business. You can create the kind of image about you that you want your audience to see.

Social Media Is Very Popular in The New Age

It is common knowledge to even non-tech readers or fans and marketing novices that social media is very popular among customers of businesses and products.

Recent research at Pew Research center shows that 65 percent of American adults are active users of social media networks. What this implies is that almost every customer that visits you is a social media user.

The Facebook network currently has a record of 1.7 billion active users in a month. For small businesses, this is easily an excellent place to start getting involved with social media marketing.

Facebook is developed in such a way that there is hardly a business that will not benefit from establishing and managing a presence there. It is very dynamic in function, user-friendly, and provides a broad and extensive audience, considering the massive number of users. Facebook is such a friendly place to start that extending from there to other social media networks will be very easy for you.

Social Media Is More Budget Friendly

Most big social media networks offer advertising packages that are easy on the budget. As a small business owner, you can take advantage of this to reach your audience and provide them with your content. These services are a good bargain for the low prices because social media networks now filter what gets to each user's feeds and your generic content may be drowned in the mix.

Traditional advertising costs more than social media methods, so this is good news since you no longer must break the bank to reach out to the public, grow your audience, and increase your business.

Social Media Encourages Two-Way Communication
On social media, you can receive feedback from your audience and learn about their interests and preferences.

You can get to know your customers better by asking questions that encourage them to share their thoughts and ideas with you. On your part, you can also give them quick responses without going through the hassles of using the phone or thinking about whether they will get your answers or not.

Social Media Users Are Consistent
One interesting thing to note about people who use social media is that they mean it in every single essence when they say they use social media. Reliable statistics have shown that in the USA alone, the average social media user checks his account 17 times in a day to catch up on news feeds.

It implies that they are more likely to receive your social media contents several times in a day and be updated on your business, even while they hardly pay any visits to your on-site location.

You Can Reveal More About Your Business on Social Media

These days, social media websites are where potential customers search when they want to learn more about a brand or a business. It is not surprising because these sites have a design that allows the business owners to share the most recent information about everything they offer from products and services to upcoming events.

Also, when someone is searching for something related tonight you offer, your business can come up as the answer to the search. It is made possible by the tools on social media that can index your activities and information by the search engines.

Social Media Is an Excellent Tool for Good Customer Service

Being able to provide good customer service is one of the strong points of any successful small business. While social media easily provides a two-way communication platform for you and your customers, it is also an excellent platform for you to improve the efficiency of your customer service and provide quick responses to your audience.

This way, it is more ensured that customer inquiries are not ignored, and your audience will be privier to the fact that you care about them and their experience with your brand.

When you establish social media for customer service and provide an instant response to their inquiries, you can meet business goals with ease. Current statistics have shown that businesses that handle their customer feedbacks well through social media earn more revenue by 20-40 percent more than others.

Social Media Improves the Efficiency of Your Email Marketing

Email marketing which is one of the ancient marketing techniques now has a new side to it because of the rise of social media. You can now cover more audience by sharing your email newsletter in all your social networks. This way, you are not limited to just your list of subscribers or followers. Your content can be seen now by a much larger and better-targeted audience, and you will get the kind of awareness that can drive sales.

You can also invite readers more readers and subscribers by adding a link on in your Facebook or other social pages for them.
Small businesses which have seized this opportunity and combined these groundbreaking tools have recorded a difference in marketing and have gotten a level playing ground to create more awareness for their business and improve their relationship with existing customers.

Everyone Uses Social Media

The larger population of Americans today uses smartphones. I'm in response to this development, a growing number of businesses are going the digital way and offering mobile-user experiences. The big social networks like Pinterest, Twitter, Instagram, and Facebook provide free to use mobile applications that enable business owners, and managers establish and maintain their online presence very easily. Small businesses indeed benefit a lot from the rising trend of mobile activity being a part of everyday life. Even better is the fact that mobile apps allow their users to connect to websites of their choice from anywhere.

User activities aren't limited to just sharing events from their personal lives. People also use their social networks to search for products, services, businesses and connect with brands.

Social media, especially when it is mobile friendly, is a great way to get awareness for your business or product because you can be found when someone is running a search on the go for something related.

Chapter 3:
Getting Started

In this chapter, we will be looking at the different strategies you can implement in growing your personal brand. These strategies are like those you incorporate in developing a business.

STRATEGIES FOR PERSONAL BRANDING

Find A Niche

A niche is a smaller part of a large industry which you choose to focus your personal brand. It is essential to select a niche to reach an audience that will have a genuine interest in what you have to offer. When selecting the right niche for your personal brand, there are a few questions you can answer:

- What do you love doing?

- Is there a group of people you enjoy working with?

- Do you prefer a specific industry?

- Can I make money in this niche?

- Is there a small part of that industry where the audience is not receiving enough attention?

- Do you think you can meet the needs of individuals within this small part?

If you can answer these questions, then you will find a good niche. I mean ALL the questions. You may be a professional lawyer, but you can't handle all types of cases. A criminal lawyer doesn't do the same job as a Personal Injury Lawyer.

During a niche selection, a lot of people make the mistake of choosing a category which will get them audiences from various areas. It voids the reason for a niche selection. The niche should be a small part of a much larger industry that will provide a targeted audience. You will not be able to appeal to anyone if you are trying to appeal to everyone. To further explain, consider an individual that performs game reviews.

The gaming industry covers sports, adventure, simulation, Massively Multiplayer Online (MMO), and many more categories. If you decide to build a brand within the gaming industry, you cannot appeal to everyone within the industry. The terms that apply to sports games differ from those that apply to MMOs.

Trying to review games from all categories implies that you will be unable to become an expert in a category. You won't be able to give an in-depth review of any category.

By focusing on a category, you can connect with the audience. Connecting with the audience will earn their trust. People will usually follow someone they trust. To be able to connect with the audience, you need to learn everything about them. You can start by answering the following questions:

- What daily struggles do they experience?

- What are the things they might think about?

- What are their beliefs?

- Is there anything that may prevent them from getting a good night's rest?

By getting to know your audience, you will be able to tailor your content to meet their needs.

Analyzing Your Competition

This analysis is in no way supposed to be a comparison. It is only a strategy which helps in identifying areas you can leverage for your success within a niche. Through this analysis, it is also possible to identify a niche that is oversaturated.

Having an excess competition and having no competition indicate that a niche is not the best option. When there is no competition, it implies that there is no target audience in need of content. Choose a niche with a few experts with a lot of room for you to grow. There should also be opportunities for your brand to stand out within the niche.

Understand Your Personal Brand

You can only know the expectations your target audience have if you have a clear understanding of the personal brand you are building. You will also can use these expectations to benefit your personal brand.

The first step is to learn what makes your brand indispensable. It can be a skill or multiple skills which your personal brand offers but no other brand does. As soon as you identify these skills, showcase them at every opportunity. Your personal brand is already being established on social media which makes it the best place to display your skills. It can be by posting helpful comments on different topics. You can also contribute to other pages in a niche that aligns with your other skills.

It is also vital you make everyone understand that you are available to help if the need arises. Always look to create opportunities for your personal brand. If you have unique skills which you are not showing to the world, you will become underrated and undervalued. It is not what you want for your personal brand. A personal brand that is underrated becomes the last option for the target audience. They do not expect much from you.

Creating A Brand Voice

The voice you choose for your personal brand determines how you interact with your audience. It also defines the response you get from the audience. There are different paths you can take when developing your brand voice. Your personal voice can be in any of the following formats:

- Authoritative

- Informative

- Friendly

- Conversational

- Technical

- Professional

As your personal brand develops, it becomes easier for the brand voice to evolve. Although this is an option, sticking to a unique brand voice is essential. The right brand voice will make it easy to form a connection with your audience.

Since your personal brand will include a lot of authentic posts, a consistent brand voice will make it easily recognizable. When your audience visits your profile on any platform, they will be expecting both a personality and a voice that is familiar.

Identify Your Target Audience

This is just a quick look since you will find a whole chapter on your target audience as you read on. The target audience is the foundation of your personal brand. It is essential you know the people you are trying to appeal to. As a personal brand, you will be able to identify your competitive advantage if you pick a target audience. It will help in improving the clarity of your brand message.

Understand the Importance of Making Connections

Your personal brand will feel the impact of the connections you make now and in the future. Creating a connection usually depends on the first impression you leave on a new member of your audience. The first thing you need to understand is that there is no do-over when it comes to first impressions.

Being intentional is an excellent way to steer an interaction to leave a good lasting impression. You can also use it to assess the image an individual has of your personal brand. Answering the following questions can help you get an idea of the impression your audience has about your brand:

- How many members of your target audience know about your personal brand?

- What do these members know about the personal brand?

- Is there anyone that doesn't know about your personal brand but can have a positive influence on the brand?

- Are you reaching individuals who can promote your brand in the future?

- Do you have a good relationship with top personal brands within your niche?

By considering the answers to these questions, it is possible to identify where you stand. Always keep this in mind when engaging with your audience. Each interaction should be able to promote your personal brand.

How Do You Establish Connections?

There are specific topics you can talk about within your niche which may give you the opportunity for a favorable interaction. Learning how to curate content to be beneficial to both your personal brand and the target audience is essential. Here is how you create great connections:

Your Profile Should Announce You

Building a personal brand will involve extensive use of various social media platforms. Each platform usually offers its users the opportunity to set up a profile. The profile contains some personal information which makes the user easy to find. When setting up your profile, it is crucial you highlight your unique skills and your niche. It makes it easy for other people within the niche to find you.

Be Informed

To make connections, having the latest information is necessary. The information you need includes any upcoming events, any online conversation within your niche, trending topics within your niche, as well as problems that need to be solved within your niche.

Learning about upcoming events and attending such events can provide the opportunity for one-on-one interactions with influencers within your niche. Posting your opinions on a trending topic will also give other online personal brands the opportunity to assess your expertise.

Make Your Own Opportunities

One of the simplest ways to create a connection is to make your own opportunities. Attending an industry event is an easy way to meet other people in the industry. Solving a common problem within your niche will also gain the attention of other personal brands and influencers within the niche. This will promote interaction with these influencers and brands.

Don't Write-Off the Competition

Your goal as a personal brand is to bring something different, a unique perspective, to the table. There is no better way to achieve this than to research the competition. The research will show you what they are doing, what they are not doing, areas of strengths as well as weakness. These are areas where you can identify pointers for improvements. You can also study the effectiveness of the processes which a competitor adopts.

Skills You Need to Develop When Building A Personal Brand

Writing Skills

Becoming an excellent writer is essential in creating a personal brand. As an excellent writer, you can curate content that will be pleasurable to your audience, offer clarity, and simplicity. You can follow any of these two paths to develop your writing skill:

- Working alongside an editor or writer with more experience: a lot of people have chosen to enlist the services of a ghostwriter when developing content. Although this method may prove to have its downsides later, it is an excellent place to start. You can opt for this method if you are having difficulties creating time to improve your personal writing skills.

- Train in writing content in English: Learning to write in plain English is the most effective way to develop your writing skills. English is a better language option since a broader audience understands it. It is also easier to find people who can translate your work to other languages if it is in English.

Become A Master at Public Speaking

To become successful in building a personal brand, you need to be confident when talking to other professionals within a niche as well as your audience. It is common for individuals to have a fear of public speaking. The most crucial step is trying to conquer this fear. Like how you perfect any other skill; you can master the art of public speaking by engaging in public speaking. By getting used to it, the fear will slowly fade away.

It is also important you don't mistake nervousness for fear. It is entirely reasonable for an individual to feel nervous before a speech. It affects even those you may consider masters in the art. To start, turn your focus to small groups. It can be in a peer support group, professional association, or a community gathering.

Effective Use Of SEO

An essential skill that a lot of people learn later is Search engine optimization. Regardless of its importance, it is relatively easy to understand. One or two days of study should be able to shape your writing.

There are still a few aspects which may be very difficult to learn, but the basics are quite easy to grasp. One of the most challenging parts of the SEO process is finding the right keywords. It must be a keyword that is relevant, has a large search volume, an easily rank at the top of google search results. There are a lot of online resources available to learn more about SEO optimization.

Email Marketing

Sending a personal email is not the same as Email marketing. A subscription to an email service provider is necessary to make use of email marketing. These providers include Constant Contact and MailChimp. To get the most out of this service, you should avoid using desktop email clients such as Outlook.

Developing your email marketing skill involves learning the basics of sending an email broadcast. You will also need a clear understanding of the analytics, segmentation, automated drip campaigns, and personalization.

Chapter 4:
Understanding Your Target Audience

What Is A Target Audience?

A target audience is a unique group of individuals who have similar characteristics. Individuals who make up this group are those who are likely going to show interest in the services or products you offer. There are different ways to narrow down your target audience. It includes any of the following:

- Income

- Gender

- Profession

- Age

- Marital status

- Location

- Level of education

Why Is It So Important?

The importance of having a target audience is quite simple. Being ef-fective in creating your content is necessary. It is more useful to appeal to a specific group of individuals with similar interests. Importance of connecting with your audience

Loyalty

Forming an understanding with your target audience is one of the best ways to gain their loyalty. Through this understanding, it is possible to learn about their needs and offer services that will cater to these needs.

Since there will be consistency in the high-quality services, your target audience keeps patronizing your brand. As your reputation grows, there will also be confidence and trust. It is how you can establish loy-alty.

Reduced Marketing Effort

An understanding between you and your audience will solidify the con-nection between both parties. As you foster this connection, it will lead to a client base consisting of your regular audience members. Having a client base minimizes the additional costs you will need to spend when marketing new services and products. Your client base will also be will-ing to assist in referring your brand to attract new customers.

Brand Advocates

Through an understanding of the basic requirements of your audience, it is easier to satisfy them. Continuous satisfaction can turn your audience into your brand advocates. As brand advocates, your audience will recommend and promote your brand to others. It means you get free marketing that increases your brand awareness and reputation.

Effective Targeting

Connecting with your audience makes it possible to advertise to them effectively. It will be easy to learn about the social media platforms they use, the kind of entertainment that interests them, and what moves them to take actions.

Through the results of your findings, it is possible to tailor your content to your audience to produce the impact you desire. Your audience will only listen if they find meaning within your message. A good connection with your audience also makes it possible to pitch new ideas to them.

How to Improve Exposure and Conversions

Contacting Niche Bloggers and Vloggers

There are lots of other social media pages that have a large following that you can connect. It can also be a vlog or a blog. If you have a product you sell, you can reach out to such individuals to make a sponsored post.

The sponsored post is another easy way to connect with other users who have an interest in your products. Although this is like what you do when building your personal brand, you are sharing your products with a fan base different from yours.

Popular sponsored posts which are available on YouTube are "unboxing" videos. Such videos show a YouTuber unbox a product, tell users about the product, and try out the product for users to see. It is a cheaper means of getting more viewers to look at your product. This method is quite affordable when considering the kind of exposure, it offers.

Using Targeted Advertisements

Social media makes it very easy to post ads online. As a result, a lot of users have become blind to most of the ads that appear. It is why you need to implement targeted advertisements. Through the interests or demographic information of users, it is possible to post an ad which will be relevant to the user. By incorporating targeted ads in your brand building strategy, you can expand your reach to a broader audience.

Using A Referral System

Networking is a crucial part of your personal brand. By growing your network, you can reach more individuals. A referral system is one of the few methods available to expand this network. In this system, users have a unique referral code that they can give out to other individuals.

By giving out this referral code, they can attract new prospects which you otherwise would not be able to reach.

There should be an incentive that will make users more likely to give out this code. It can be in the form of a discount on their next purchase or a commission. Regardless of what form the offer takes, it should be valuable enough to prompt users to share the code. A low offer will not provide the motivation that users need. As a result, you may have a low yield.

Partnering with Other Brands

Your personal brand can gain a lot from a partnership with a larger company in the market. The company doesn't have to compete with your brand. The good idea is to pick a company that complements the services you offer your viewers.

In a way, the partnership must be mutually beneficial to both parties. An easy way to explain this partnership is to consider a YouTuber who performs video game reviews on YouTube. This individual may have the opportunity to partner with a larger gaming studio that provides certain resources. It can be in the form of free versions of a new game while the YouTuber offers a gameplay review to subscribers. There are other forms of partnership which are a lot easier to understand.

Attend Events

Most of the work you will be doing when building your personal brand will be online. Nonetheless, you should also remember to take advantage of traditional methods. In this case, look out for events around you that you can attend. The event may be a festival, convention, seminar, or conference where you can display your products and services. Directly engaging with other participants during such events can be very beneficial.

Guest Blogging

Establishing yourself as an expert creates a lot of openings for you to grow your audience. One of such openings is the opportunity to become a guest blogger. Guest blogging is a method through which you increase traffic to your site by writing a content which you post on another blog. The blog you write for will usually be one which is within your niche.

The main benefit of guest blogging is that you gain access to the viewers on the blog where you post the content. You also can post links that redirect back to your site. If you decide to participate in guest blogging, quality is paramount. The quality of the content you are posting on the blog should be of high standards to attract new viewers to your blog. It is also vital you guest blog on blogs that have targeted following.

Creating written content is more common, but there are a few companies that may want videos. You should jump at these opportunities. The exposure you get from videos is usually a lot more than written content offers.

How to Identify Opportunities to Grow Your Audience

When you need to identify opportunities for audience growth, it can be through quantitative or qualitative research.

Quantitative Research

It is a form of research which depends on numerical data. The research offers an opportunity for you to learn about the strengths of competitors as well as the weaknesses you can use to your advantage.

Quantitative research provides opportunities to find areas where you can grow your audience from better understanding of customer demographics. Although it usually contains a lot of statistical information, it is crucial you don't rely solely on the data. You need to combine the other forms of information available to make more beneficial changes. Quantitative research includes the following:

- Product sales number

- Financial trends

- Questionnaires

Qualitative Research

Qualitative research is an easy way to learn about customer interests, trends in the industry which have been poorly implemented, as well as attitudes and views of customers. You can perform qualitative research through any of the following methods:

- A review of your competitors to learn about their customer services as well as products

- Creating focus groups that consist of both potential customers as well as you true customers

- Conversations, both formal and informal, with your customers

Qualitative research data is not as easy to interpret as quantitative research data. By identifying the trends, you can implement, it is possible to attract more clients to your personal brand. To further understand how to gain information from quantitative and qualitative research, you should assess different areas of your personal brand.

Assessing Your Audience

To understand the behavior of your prospects, it is crucial you assess your audience. Some of the information you will gain from this assessment include how your brand influences the audience, how the audience evaluates your brand, and how they get information regarding the brand. To assess your audience, you need to combine various research methods such as:

- Surveys and interviews of customers

- Analytics

- Keyword research

- Analysis of user-generated content

- Brand immersion

With these methods, it is possible to create a profile for an individual within the audience. It also allows you to adjust your strategy to suit the profile.

Assessing the Trends

When developing your content strategy, the "what" aspect is important. Evaluating the trends can help in the definition of this aspect.

During this assessment, you will need to gather contents with the most engagement within your niche and analyze this content. You will also need to analyze patterns in this content. Once your analysis is complete, it is possible to identify areas where you can improve your content strategy to attract more of your target audience. Here are some methods which are beneficial when assessing trends:

- Analysis of resources cited

- Identifying subtopics

- Sentiment analysis

- Analysis of quoted experts

- Determining the angle

- Analysis of compelling questions

Through these research methods, it becomes possible to understand what makes why your target audience interacts with content, questions they are likely to answer, as well as content they share and cite.

Assessing the Media
By evaluating the media, you can discover other personal brands within your niche that attract the most of your target audience. Combining the results of your media assessment to the results of your trends assessment, you have a better understanding of how to develop content that will gain the attention of the audience.

- Assessing the media should include the following methods:

- Analysis of social engagement

- Analysis of industry experts

- Analysis of paid media

- Analysis of social influencers in your industry

- Analysis of industry publications

All these are content sources in an industry. By analyzing these sources, you can promote your content more effectively.

Assessing the Competition

Both in business and a personal brand, there is always a competitor. Your competition is the main reason why you are making your brand unique.

By assessing the competition, you can spot new opportunities for growth that is not being leveraged by your competitors. Assessing the competition includes the following:

- Evaluating SEO optimization

- Analyzing the navigation and architecture of social media pages

- Content inventory

- Analysis of keyword gap

Through the competition assessment, you can better understand the reason for specific actions.

How to Assess the Competition

To successfully evaluate your competition, you need to identify the competition. You need to have a list of these competitors. Creating this list is quite easy – look for personal brands within the niche you have chosen. The next step is to identify the strengths and weaknesses of each competitor. It involves taking note of what makes each competitor unique, the services or experience they offer their audience and areas where they are lacking.

Taking note of the keywords each competitor is using and those they avoid can also be very helpful. Also, identify the platforms where their audience can find them and those where they have no presence. Now that you have done your research on the competition, it is time to look at your brand. What are the things that you can do differently? What strengths do you have that separate you from your competition?

You should have a separate slide for each competitor, so your work is easy. List all the findings under each competitor and state your recommendations on how to make your brand better. The date of the research is crucial. So much can change in a short time.

A Quick Summary

Growth opportunities for your audience become easy to identify when you spot the needs of your target audience which are not currently being satisfied by your personal brand or other brands within your niche.

Your ability to notice growing trends in the form of weak signals will also be useful in leveraging an opportunity before it blooms into a more significant trend on which your competition can jump on. Niche communities, social listening, and industry buzz can help in noticing these weak signals.

Chapter 5:
How to Make Your Brand Unique

For you to stand out from the crowd, the first step is to accept the things that make you unique. It is common to find a lot of people with unique traits that blend with the crowd. Others create an image for themselves and stand out.

It is essential you avoid shaping your persona to fit societal labels. Accepting the things that make you different will make it possible to control how your life. There are different areas where individuals are unique. These aspects can also help in shaping the brand they develop. Some of the important aspects include the following:

Experiences
The experiences an individual will have throughout their lifetime will differ from those any other individual will have. It doesn't matter if you grow up in the same home or spend a lot of time together with a person.

Your experiences in life also serve as huge turning points as you grow. It can be your biggest failure, your most embarrassing moment, a choice you make, or a moment when you had your most significant success. These experiences shape the person you have become and are some of the things that make you unique.

Creativity

It is another important aspect which makes each person unique. The creative ability of an individual is entirely different from the other. In some individuals, it is the ability to invent a new product while in others, it is the ability to develop a way to carry out a task.

Creativity can be further subdivided into talents that include the vision-ary, inventor, adventurer, pilot, explorer, navigator, poet, and diplomat. This is according to Lynne Levesque, Ed. D.

Perception

Everyone has a unique perception of life. It is a unique way you view different happenings around you. It also affects the experiences you will have.

Creating A Brand That Is Unique

Make a list of the exclusive offers your brand has for its clients. Let your offer to the market distinguish you from other brands including those with higher capitals. For your brand to stand out in the very com-petitive market of today, you need to carry out a careful study of what society requires that no one is offering. Pay rapt attention to the quality of the product and services your brand has to offer.

The first step to take is to carefully select your target audience and give them something different from what other similar brands as yours are offering. Even better, let your services and product be in line with improving the lives of your customers in ways such as;

- Providing better options at an affordable rate

- Improved customer service

- Improving productivity

- Stress relieves on daily activity

- Time management

Let there be a balance among knowledge, passion, and profitability. You hear people talk about choosing a niche to focus like it is something straightforward to do. There is a wide range of niches one can decide to focus on, but it could be a little bit of a challenge to find one that catches your interest, you're knowledgeable in, and you can monetize. Therefore, before choosing a niche to focus on ensure those critical factors are not missing.

Be Different but Real

Let your brand show people the real you; this is because no matter how hard you try people can always identify fake. Other than doing what every other person is doing, think of new outstanding ideas and offer it to the society.

Ask yourself a question, if you quit today what would be the reaction of your customers. What is that unique offer of yours your customer would miss the most when you decide to quit today? Your answer to this question is the most valuable selling point of your brand.

Be Human

There is more to it than just standing out, be human as well. It is essential to see your client and competitor as the humans they are, therefore strive to build a good customer relationship with the clients.

Do Not Be Overly Money Conscious

Instead of choosing your area of focus based on money, do something you love. It might take a long while to monetize your passion, but it's sure better than forcing yourself to belong to a niche you know nothing about and have zero passion for. It will save you from wasting time and effort and probably ending up depressed and worn out.

Do Not Force It

It could be tempting to follow a trend and what others are doing but that might not play out well for you. It is best to focus on something you are well grounded in and passionate about; this will give you a better chance at achieving success.

Stay True to Yourself

Reach out to people already in the same niche you wish to go into, learn from them and share the knowledge you have with them as well. Show the world the real you and what you have to offer. Do not imitate or try to be like someone else; originality is key to success. If you feel you can't survive in a niche choose another.

Create Your Buyer Persona

Do not be a "jack of all trade, master of none" kind of brand. It is better to have one job correctly done than have several poor ones. Maintaining focus on one thing gives trust in your brand. To do this, you can get free templates online that would help you create a good buyer persona for your clients.

Decide on what your Value-Add would be. Identify that unique skill or quality you possess that will make your brand stand out and capitalize on it. Every individual has something unique about them, figure yours out and offer it to the society.

Talk to Those Close to You

It is easier to know more about yourself, your strength and weakness from those closest to you. Talk to your colleagues, friends, and family and find out what they think about you. Request that they be plain with you and hold nothing back. By so doing you would come to discover things you probably didn't know about yourself.

Know and Trust in Yourself

We sometimes pass through the trial and error process to decide which niche to focus on. Base your decision on passion, skill, and knowledge. The moment this is determined, work with it and create a unique brand that truly defines you.

Personalize It

A unique brand is most often than not personal. It defines the face behind the brand, the individual's communication skills, interest, values
and lots more. Your brand must have something captivating to offer to
the public, or you leave them indifferent towards you. Always apply this
rule to your business, "stand apart by standing out."

Analyze Your Competitors

Study your competitors, find out what they are currently talking about,
what is trending online and what the market expects from your sector.
Go deeper into topics other brands are ignoring and create something
unique out of it for your brand.

Who Are You?

Do not alter your identity to fit in; no one can be more you than you. If
you wish to retain your customers or client, it is essential that you stay
genuine to yourself as people can easily see through fakeness. Do not
lose yourself in a bid to do what others are doing.

Create A Unique Blueprint for Your Brand

Creating the perfect blueprint for your brand that will speak to your
audience and tell them who you are, there are three important exer-
cises you must carry out. First, make a list of what the market needs
the most, then make a list of your best skills, and finally make a list of
your greatest passion. Create your brand blueprint around the top

choices from each list. Below is a list of areas every business should focus on for growth.

Channel Strengths

Create a platform whereby people can easily access your brand; your availability should play out in your favor. Seeks out other options that would help widen your reach online, you can try promoting your brand on various social media channel. A change in environment or platform could be the change your platform needs to move forward. However, because change brings about different reactions to ensure that your content is of high value or you risk losing your customers.

Product Strength

Rather than focusing majorly on technical supremacy, pay more attention to the quality of your product. The quality of your product will speak better for your brand and keep you ahead of others in your industry. When people build trust in your brand as a result of the quality services you offer, you become a force to be reckoned with.

People Strengths

Think of those qualities that made you choose your employees and use it to your advantage. Encourage them to put in more effort and do better than they have in the past. Figure out ways by which you can bring out the best in them to achieve the desired result. You can accomplish this by giving them a more complex task than they have previously handled. Study your team, find out their strength and maximize it to the advantage of your brand. Hire an HR team with the capacity to choose very efficient employees.

Competitive Strengths

Raise the bar so high that your competitors will struggle to measure up with. However, you need a team of highly efficient people to pull this through. Give your team the task to achieve an outrageous vision within a limited period. Let this task be an upgrade to the brand vision that you need to implement rather than as a new goal. It will cause your team to figure out better strategies to achieve this and in turn help build individual strength. Provide useful resources and opportunities for your team and train them on how to handle the task ahead. It gives your team the impression that what you require of them is achievable. Build the strength of your brand from the inside to achieve the desired result.

Awareness Strengths

Give the market something specific to make them remember you. With the high rate of competition in the world today, it requires significant effort to stand. Study your target market and your competitors and find out what you can do to make your brand preferable to others. Do something that will increase your visibility on social media platforms. Stay active on the channels where you experience better visibility and let your presence be felt. Find out the areas of your business that requires improvement to boost your visibility. Focus on inclination more than demographics.

Adaptive Strengths

Do you find it easy to adapt to changes? If yes, in what ways can you best utilize this attribute to the betterment of your business? Identifying and accepting changes rapidly can be an added advantage to your business especially if you specialize in a highly competitive niche. It will make your brand stand out as that brand that brings about the change the market desires. Your brand is appreciated for daring to move along with the trend, and your customers are usually the first to benefit from this change. Therefore, because you were bold enough to bring about change you become a leading brand in your industry and command the respect of others. It is vital to ensure you do not move faster than appropriate all in the bid to over-impress people; this could hurt your brand. Moving along with trend gives you the edge to get investors who are looking to invest in something new. Your pace to adapting to changes must be beneficial to your cause, or you stand the risk of falling out.

Chapter 6:
Creating A Personal Brand on YouTube

What Is YouTube?

On the internet today, YouTube remains the most popular video sharing platform available. As a registered user on the platform, you will have the opportunity to share video content. Anyone who visits the site will be able to access and watch the videos. Some of the key functions of YouTube include the following:

- Uploading videos to a channel

- Using keywords to search for videos

- Watching videos

- Posting comments, liking, and sharing videos from other users

- Creating playlists of similar videos

- Subscribing to YouTube Channels

- Gaining subscribers on your channel

What Makes YouTube Useful?

As a video sharing platform which is free to use, YouTube offers a lot of educational videos. It is a platform where users can discover new ideas. Helpful, instructional videos are also available for users. Some of the video contents available on the site include how-to guides, hacks, music videos, recipes, comedy shows, game reviews, and more. It is also a great platform for vloggers to showcase their creativity.

THE VALUE OF YOUTUBE

It Offers A Large Traffic

YouTube remains one of the most important online video sharing platforms available. Daily, people view over 3 billion videos on the platform. It is a clear indication of the traffic on the platform.

Using YouTube to build your personal brand also implies that you will have access to this high traffic. It also becomes effortless to reach your target audience. There are other significant advantages which you can enjoy from the traffic on YouTube. These include the following:

- The ease with which you can locate your target audience and individuals who are likely going to become your fans

- There are over 1 billion users who pay to enjoy YouTube videos every month

- It becomes easier for people to locate your personal brand as it is the 2nd largest search engine in the world

- Maintaining consistency and offering high-quality content which solves a significant issue of a viewer will earn their loyalty

It Improves Your Visibility on Google

If you type in a keyword into a Google search panel, you will notice that videos also come up. The Google search results are usually a combination of these videos along with images, books, news, and more. It is a good way to ensure that you find the most relevant information available on the internet.

The number of videos that show up alongside text-only pages goes to show how important videos are becoming. In building your personal brand, YouTube can help you take advantage of this growing trend.

The best way to leverage this opportunity is to create high-quality written content which you can then complement with a high-quality video on YouTube. The written content may be on your blog or social media platform with a direct link to your YouTube page. It will increase your personal brand appearance on Google search results. Incorporating YouTube into your personal brand building strategy will also establish your brand authority within your niche. Setting yourself as an expert will even get you noticed by Google. It then makes it possible for your page ranking on search results to rise.

Re-purposing Your Content

Re-purposing content is very beneficial since it helps in saving both time and money. It is also very efficient when you are trying to market your content. It is a lot easier to reach your target audience since it is the type of content that meets their specifications. If you run a blog, some of the formats that are available for re-purposing content include:

- Video Series

- Podcasts

- Presentations

Through re-purposing of content, you can develop a single idea into about four content formats. It makes it possible to reach a wider audience with improvements in engagement.

YouTube Helps You Create an Email List

Providing content which is valuable and engaging offers an opportunity to increase your email list. You can find a software that allows users sign-up to the email list from the video. This software will stop the video for a short time so that the user can add an email address to subscribe to the list.

It is an easy and stress-free method of growing your email list. Remember, it will only be useful if you offer high-quality and engaging content.

Your Viewers Will Help in Promoting You and Purchase from You. Conversions are possible through videos on YouTube. If there is a personal touch that connects with the viewer, they are more likely going to make a purchase. Connecting with them on an emotional scale will build trust between both parties.

It Offers the Option to Monetize Your Channel

Using Google AdSense video program is an easy way to earn money you're your YouTube videos. It is usually available if you can consistently upload high-quality videos. The earnings on your channel can enter six-figures annually if you use it correctly. It is a combination of your earnings from the Google AdSense as well as what you aid from paid adverts. Don't think you are the first to learn about AdSense – there are over 20 million YouTube channels already benefitting from the program.

Become A Global Sensation

The reach you get from YouTube is quite phenomenal. Since it is a video sharing platform, people from various parts of the world find it easy to identify your brand. Authorizing support for subtitles on YouTube will also allow you to share content with viewers regardless of the language barrier. Consistently uploading videos will open doors for new viewers from these locations. The option of including a closed caption will also enable you to connect with viewers with unique requirements.

Closed captions have become an essential part of YouTube videos. According to research, videos with closed caption have a 4% increase in the number of views and subscribers. Including a Call-to-Action is a great way to promote your personal brand through YouTube. Adding links to other videos, services, and other social pages also help.

You Will Have More Visibility on Search Engines

Since Google includes videos and images to its search results, YouTube can help improve the visibility of your personal brand. Uploading videos regularly with new content in each video will improve your chances of appearing in a search result.

Proper use of metadata is one factor that affects the outcome in this case. Google and other search engines pick up metadata when selecting results which will be relevant to the search entry. Creating a blog post on a topic and then providing a link to the video is also very helpful. The link should direct the viewers to your YouTube channel.

CREATING A STRONG YOUTUBE PRESENCE

Promote

Another way to drive traffic to your YouTube channel is by promoting the channel on other social media platforms. The first step is to post short clips on different social media profiles. If the video offers high-quality content, viewers will be looking to watch it till the end.

Adding a link is also important. It is the only way you can redirect the traffic to your channel. It also prevents the competition from getting the attention of your viewers while they try to locate your channel.

You should also get your viewers to subscribe to your channel. It improves the chances of your videos appearing on the YouTube homepage. Including metadata will also promote video optimization. Add keywords to these descriptions to enhance effectiveness. Video optimization also promotes your channel on Google as they become more noticeable in search results.

Selecting A Featured Video

Your featured video is the first video that appears to any user that opens your channel homepage. Why not make it your best? It is important you choose a video which has a high-quality recording, is relevant, entertaining, and short. These features are self-explanatory. To appeal to users, you should try to change this video often. A title that attracts viewers is also crucial for your featured video. A thumbnail which best depicts the video is also essential.

Customize Your Channel

The appearance of your channel can also make it unique. The aesthetic you choose when customizing the channel should reflect the brand. Colors and logos that your audience can associate with your brand should be used in the videos.

Create A Schedule

While building your personal brand, you may not have enough resources to hire people to manage your social media accounts. So, you must make the most of your time.

Creating a schedule and following it will help in creating content which is fresh and of high-quality. It, in turn, attracts the target audience you have in mind. Starting a series of how-to videos makes it easy to come up with a new idea for the next video. It also attracts the target audience in anticipation for the next video in the series.

Reply Comments

On YouTube, users can comment after a video or also drop a comment on the homepage of your channel. Administrators on YouTube have the power to disable comments, moderate them, or allow the comments. It applies to both a video and the channel.

To moderate a comment after it has been posted, you can remove it from the comments section or report as spam. Keep an eye on the comments below your videos or the channel homepage. It makes it possible to identify conversations that deserve a response. There should be a standard for deleting comments. Just because a comment is negative doesn't mean it shouldn't be on the post. Removing comments with foul language or words that are offensive is allowed.

Put Related Content in A Playlist

When a user is searching for any content that is relevant to the video they just finished watching, a playlist can assist. The playlist allows users to access another video content on the channel page easily. Through the playlist, it is possible for a viewer to keep watching videos without having to select the play button on the page. Creating labels that accurately describe the content of the videos within a playlist is very important.

Use the Analytics

On your YouTube channel, there is analytics. It includes engagement data such as the number of shares, comments, likes, and so on. Performance data and demographic data are also available on a per-video basis. Taking time to assess the information can help you decide on the usefulness of the content on your channel. It also helps to determine areas where you can make improvements to attract more subscribers and viewers.

Niche Selection Strategies

Selecting a niche for your YouTube channel is another aspect you need to cover. Having a good niche strategy is also essential if you want to avoid making any decision you may regret later. In this section, you will find some useful tips which you can use in shaping your niche selection strategy.

What Do You Have A Passion For? What Are You Great At?

Your passion is always an excellent focus on your channel. It is an area where you are likely going to have the most experience as well as confidence.

You can start by listing out all the things you do well. Areas where you show exceptional talent should be at the top of this list. It is an excellent time to be proud of some all these talents. Being an expert in a field may not be the focus when selecting a niche. It should be a subtle blend of your talents and your passion that will decide a niche where you will stand out. As you begin to build yourself within a niche, you will slowly grow to become an expert.

When you sit down and think about a video, how many topics come to mind? Any number less than ten shows that this is not the best niche for you. It only shows that getting inspiration to run the channel within that niche will be very difficult. Are there changes that will affect your passion for this niche? Is it a passion that will change in a few years? Assessing your answers to this question can help you better understand your passion.

A video that is useful to a subscriber will make them visit more often. You may consider building a channel within the entertainment niche. Although viewers may enjoy getting a good laugh, they will still opt for a channel that can provide useful information they can apply to their daily activities. Channels that make the most money are usually those that provide information which both investors and viewers consider being helpful.

Does Your Potential Niche Have an Audience?

If you can pick out a niche that you are moving towards, you must ensure that there are people who will watch your videos. It means that there should be a target audience for the niche. There will be certain subjects you will need to cover within a niche. Is there an audience searching for these topics? If there is, then you are going to get people to view your videos. You should perform quick research to see how much people search for the niche you have chosen. An excellent place to start is the Google AdWords Keyword Planner. It shows the monthly searches which a keyword gets on the average.

Google Trends is another vital tool. It shows the popularity of a topic over a period. With this tool, you can know if a niche is only popular at a specific time during the year as well as changes in demand with time.

What Is the Competition Like Within the Niche and What Do They Offer?

The competition in a niche will determine the difficulty when building your brand within the niche. A simple look at the number of active YouTubers within the niche will give you a clear idea. A niche that is full of YouTubers will be challenging when starting. Being flexible with your niche choices will make it easy to find one with less competition. It is crucial that the niche is in high demand. So, you are searching for a low competition with high demand niche in this case.

If you are already building a personal brand on other social media platforms, this is not an option. Using targeting keywords will help in a competitive niche. Although things will be a lot more difficult, you can still reach your goals. You also need to analyze what the other YouTubers in the niche are doing. Learn about the content they offer. Also, learn how they promote engagement on their channel. Reading through comments from their audience can show you some of the flaws in their content and where you can make improvements. You must remain authentic and unique in your approach.

How Will You Stand Out Within the Niche?

High-quality content is not enough to keep your viewers interested. You must be skillful in how you make the presentation. Making the content fun for your viewers is also vital.

Your viewers will drop you for someone who offers the same high-quality content but with more entertainment. Adding some personality to your videos will make it unique and more entertaining. Some easy steps to take to add entertainment to a video include:

- Working on your introduction

- Improving the way, you speak

- Your appearance

- The concept of the video

- Visual effects

Making a few changes to these areas can bring a new theme and style to your videos. You need to be very creative in making changes if you want to stand out from your competition.

How Profitable Is the Niche?

Although your initial goal is to create your brand, making money from this brand is the long-term goal. It is why you need to consider the profitability of a niche before selecting one.

- Is there any side hustle available within the niche?

- Are there companies willing to sponsor the use and review of their products?

These are questions that can help you determine a niche that will be profitable. Receiving a sponsorship is not as easy as it sounds. Nonetheless, it is precious if you can land one. You can choose to become an affiliate as a side hustle which will earn you passive income.

Using the Trends

The visibility of your videos as well as the number of views can increase significantly if the content relates to a trending topic. Since a lot of viewers will be searching for trending topics daily, you are sure to get noticed by a lot of users. With trending topics, the earlier you use it to your advantage, the better. Since users may learn a lot about the subject within a day or two, the trend may die out before you can attract viewers. Below are some of the steps you can follow to get the most out of a trend:

Use Metadata

Adding metadata to a video is possible when you are about to upload the video on YouTube. The metadata is information relating to the video such as the title, tags, and description. Including the trending keyword in each metadata will promote the visibility of the video.

Find A Way to Increase Engagement

One of the main benefits of a trending topic is that it offers the opportunity to improve engagement with your viewers. Engagement is also an easy way to increase viewership and subscriptions. Simply asking a question or making a request during the video can get you the engagement you desire. Simple statements such as:

- How do you feel about this development? Leave a comment for us to know your thoughts

- If you love this video, remember to subscribe so you can be the first to learn about new posts!

Improving the Ranking of Your Videos

As the largest video sharing platform, there are various stats which make YouTube seem difficult for new channels. The platform has many videos and channels. To create equilibrium, it also has many users and visitors. So how do you make sure you reach your audience during a search? Your video needs to have a lot of likes, views, and shares for it to appear at the top of the results during a search. It is how the YouTube algorithm identifies trending content.

Steps to Take to Improve Your Video Ranks

There are some steps you can take to push your videos up the rankings. These steps will increase the views, likes, and shares which your video will get. As soon as there is a growth in these numbers, it becomes easy to notice an increase in the video rankings.

Offer High-Quality Content

Content is the most critical factor when developing a personal brand. It remains a crucial factor across all social media platforms. You can quickly identify the importance of great content by watching some of the top videos on YouTube. After watching these videos, you will notice that they have high-quality content which attracts the audience, improves engagement through comments and likes, while also promoting shares and subscription.

The only way you will be motivated to make more high-quality videos is when you can get more views on a previous post. By offering great content, you are going to solidify your relationship with your audience over a long period. In a case where there is significant competition in your niche, you can only stand out and survive by offering high-quality content in your videos. In simpler terms, the information you provide, scripts, flow, facts, and video quality need to be the best. It doesn't matter if your videos focus on humor, games, reviews, or makeup. By providing excellent video content, you can connect easily with your target audience.

Short Videos Are Better

Do you create videos that last an hour? Who will be willing to watch a video for that long? Unless it's a movie, you won't be able to grab the attention of your target audience. It is common knowledge that the attention span of individuals nowadays is quite short so why not use it to your advantage? Developing the first minute of your video to contain a lot of high-quality information is also essential. If you are unable to make an impression in the first minute, your viewer will move on to the next before you have that opportunity again. When building a personal brand on YouTube, you need to start with short videos. As the number of subscribers begins to increase, you can that gradually increase the duration of your videos. At this time, you have already gained the trust of your viewers.

Incorporate SEO

Through SEO optimization, it becomes easier for people to find your channel in the search results. Although the way you implement SEO optimization may differ in the content format, it still has the same effect. When uploading videos to your YouTube channel, you need to create your title according to SEO standards. It is also essential you add a description, URL, and tags to the video. It is the easiest way to enhance the ranking of your video.

Come Up with A Unique Concept

Delivering fresh content is the only way you are going to retain the loyalty of your audience. No one will be able to remain loyal to a page that keeps posting a video that they have seen so many times. Regardless of the humor, entertainment, or emotions, a video can produce at first; its effects will dwindle when you view it a second or third time.

It is common to find a lot of YouTubers who stepped into the limelight due to a unique concept which they incorporated. It is also very common to see a lot of other people trying to replicate these concepts to get them into the spotlight. It is a severe error which a lot of people make. Just because it produced the right results with a person doesn't imply that it will work for you. A significant downside to taking this line of action is the loss of authenticity when developing your content.

Another significant downside to copying others is the loss of members of your audience. The members you lose in this case may never return to your channel again. A lot of people may feel that this limits their ability to grow. It is a common misconception that arises when the competition is high within a niche. All you need is to ensure you have the proper experience, create your concept and style which separates you from the competition.

Look for Ways to Increase Your Subscribers

Your subscribers also play a crucial role in your video rankings. Having many subscribers will increase the number of shares, views, and likes on your videos. It will, in turn, improve the ranking of your video. It is essential you put in more effort to get people to subscribe to your channel. Reminding viewers subscribe to your channel and like your videos is important.

Chapter 7:
Creating A Personal Brand on Facebook

Getting Started

Should you build your personal brand with a Facebook Profile or Facebook Page? The answer to this question will depend on your preferences. There are certain areas where a Facebook Page offers advantages over a Facebook profile. It is also true when the roles are reversed.

When comparing organic reach and paid reach, using a Facebook profile offers a higher organic reach. A Facebook page is a better option when it comes to paid reach. You should also note that access to paid reach and advertising is no longer available on Facebook profiles. Facebook Pages also provide the analytics option to users. Analytics on Facebook is available in the form of Facebook Insights. The Insights tab is only available on the Pages.

Attracting your target audience also varies for both. Interaction with your target audience is much more comfortable with a Facebook profile. It gives you the option of interacting with friends and even converse with people who are in a group. Having many fans is vital for a Facebook

Page. It is only through engagement and a large fan base that a Facebook page can impress your target audience. A Facebook profile also provides interaction with the target audience.

If you need access to the various parts of Facebook, a profile is your best option. You can interact with other users on Facebook pages, groups, or profiles. With a Facebook page, you can post a comment in a group or on different profiles.

SETTING UP YOUR ACCOUNT

Optimize What Everyone Can See

Four parts of your Facebook account are visible to all other Facebook users. By making information from these parts' public, Facebook makes it very easy for other users to find your account. These parts are the:

- Profile picture

- Timeline cover photo

- Name of your Facebook profile that appears at the top

- Account URL or Facebook custom username

By taking the time to customize these areas, you can get more users to view your account. Here are steps to take to optimize your account: a name that is easy to remember.

When setting up your profile, Facebook requires users to do so using their real name. Nonetheless, users get to decide the name that appears at the top part of the profile. A nickname that is easy to remember and defines your brand is an excellent option in this case.

Profile Photo

Since there is no privacy protection setting for this profile photo, it is visible to all Facebook users. It is important that the picture you choose is professional and friendly. You can use a picture of yourself at an event that relates to your brand.

A Distinct Username

The number of Facebook users worldwide makes it challenging to choose a username. It is why you need to get creative. Come up with unique a name which is meaningful to your personal brand. You also need a username which you can incorporate into your business card, email signature, and URL.

Timeline Cover Photo

As soon as a user opens your page, the cover photo is the first image they see. It covers a large part of the screen. There are lots of benefits you can gain if you use the right cover photo. To set up a great cover photo, you should use a banner size of 851 x 315 pixels. The image should also reflect your brand.

STEPS TO TAKE WHEN BUILDING YOUR PERSONAL BRAND ON FACEBOOK

Adjust Your Privacy Settings.

There is a limit to the type of contents you can allow on your page. Since you are building a personal brand, you first must decide if a piece of information should be on your Facebook page. The privacy settings on Facebook allow you to set up restrictions on your page. These restrictions include limiting access to parts of your accounts to only Facebook friends. There are other parts which need to be accessible by all Facebook users. Building a personal brand means you need to make new connections. Information about your education, work, and success should be open to the public. It makes it possible to attract people who share your interests and those who work in a similar field.

The privacy settings also help you control what posts users can tag back to your page. Tagging on Facebook allows users to link a post directly to another account. Blocking the tagging feature doesn't prevent a post from appearing on the platform. Nonetheless, it becomes complicated for your followers to relate it to your page. It is also vital you avoid leaking too much personal information.

What Is Your Story?

The main reason why you are starting a personal brand is to influence other users. There should be a story behind it. It is a story you must be willing to tell. Anyone who decides to follow your personal brand will want to be a part of the brand. One way to make them feel like a part is to let them know the story behind the brand.

A story that offers both encouragement and motivation have the most impact. These are two things your followers need you to provide. Why you are taking this path and your experiences along the line help in shaping your story, and allows your followers to get familiar with you, while also making it easier for them to follow your brand all the way.

Avoid Spamming

Spamming is very common on Facebook, and most Facebook users hate it. I said most since I can't speak for people who spam. To prevent spamming, Facebook also tries its best to improve some of the security features available on the platform. Nonetheless, you should avoid making your contents look like spam when building a personal brand on Facebook. According to the terms of service on Facebook, you need permission for third-party advertisements on pages. It is why you need to take care when posting links on your page.

Another way you may be appearing as a spammer is by being inauthentic. It may be a simple error of sharing too many links or articles without verifying the authenticity of the source. It may also be as a result of articles which you post which may be an edit of a previous article you have written. Posting different URLs to the same article is also a form of spamming. You need to make sure you don't make such mistakes.

Expand Your Network

Expanding your network is always a vital part of building your personal brand on a social media platform. On Facebook, it is possible to import new contacts from your phonebook. Other channels like instant messenger and email accounts also offer this feature. Repeating this process every month is an easy way to add more followers to your Facebook profile.

Visual Branding

In a period where there are social media platforms that support only image sharing, you cannot underestimate the power of great visuals. A significant aspect of personal branding on Facebook is your visuals. It should be able to connect your users to your brand. The use of different visuals on each social media platform is a mistake most people make. When building your personal brand, your viewers should be able to identify your brand due to its consistency. It should be the same regardless of the platform.

Having a template can be very helpful. This way you can make sure that the images you share on Facebook are consistent with those on other platforms. A lot of personal brands on social media make use of free tools like Canva to create templates. Sharing a lot of images is another way to get the attention of other users on Facebook. Since the platform depends on your ability to combine images with texts, you should be able to follow it up with a high-quality write-up.

Using Facebook Live

Facebook live offers a means to interact with your followers and meet potential followers. It helps in solidifying the relationship between your personal brand and your fans. It is a streaming video in which you can get personal and creative by providing engaging content.

One of the significant benefits of Facebook Live is how easy you can reach your viewers. All your viewer needs to do is to scroll past your Live video to connect. Once the viewer connects, they have the option of easily posting likes, emojis, and comments. The participation of your viewers is all in real-time.

How to Get the Most of This Feature

The main reason why Facebook users love Facebook Live is the authenticity of the videos. A non-professional feed usually lets your viewers see the real you. A little bit of movement here and there is okay since no one is expecting a video of professional quality. To improve the quality of your Facebook Live videos to an acceptable quality, there are certain aspects you need to improve. The first step is to get a Smartphone which offers good quality video recording. Purchasing a high-end mobile device will provide improvements in both performances as well as better video resolution.

You should also invest a reasonable amount in purchasing a tripod. A tripod offers stability over the use of a selfie stick. Narrating your story while trying to balance a selfie stick can be an arduous task. Tripods are available at various prices with some mini tripods at prices below $25. Nonetheless, it is crucial you find a tripod that is lightweight and portable. Another essential step is to pick a good location when recording a video. The place should have excellent lighting. Direct sunlight behind you is your best bet.

Getting Traffic

To get the most traffic on your Facebook Live Videos, it is essential you create a schedule for your videos. The videos should be on at a time when most of your viewers will be online. It can be when they are on their mobile device or computer. Having a video description is also essential. People should be able to know your guest, your location, what makes the video interesting, and what you will be doing without watching the videos. It is also a more natural way to get new viewers to view your Facebook Live Videos.

Interaction with your audience is a vital aspect of the live video. Getting your audience to reply by commenting and liking your feed can also boost your traffic. During the video, ensure you ask questions. The video becomes more exciting and fun for your users when they are actively participating in what is happening. As I mentioned earlier, you must be authentic. No one is willing to waste time to see a video with a script like a commercial. Produce video content that shows you now and makes it feel like live action.

A sign of appreciation goes a long way when building a personal brand. Remember to do this after saving the video to your feed. It can be a simple "thank you" comment on the video. Remember also to make use of call to action. You can use this to divert traffic to your other social media pages. Just ask your audience to follow you on Twitter, visit your blog, or like your video on Instagram. Facebook Live video is one key tool to help in personal branding since it is free to use.

Using Facebook Insights
Creating content that will interest your audience is a lot easier if you have information on their behavior. Facebook Insights offers the information you need. It provides data which you can use in improving the performance of your personal brand. To gain access to the Facebook Insights on your page, click on the "Insights" at the top of the page. There are lots of tabs which the Insights page offers to Facebook users.

Overview
The first important area to visit is the Overview tab. It offers a page summary and shows metrics for the five most current posts on your page. It also compares other Facebook Pages which are like yours. These are the areas where you can analyze using the overview tab:

- Pages to Watch

- Page summary

- Most Recent Posts

Pages to Watch

The Pages to Watch is one of the great features of Facebook Insights. It is a simple tool which helps in comparing your page to other similar pages. These pages are some of the pages which you need to monitor. It is beneficial in showing how your page is doing against other personal brands in your niche. Clicking on any of the pages will give you a ranking of the posts.

Page Summary

If you want to learn about the key metrics of the Facebook Page, you should visit the Page Summary section. It shows the Reach, Page Likes, and Post Engagement for the past week. There is also a graph to compare changes between the past and the current period. Assessing the performance of your Page with this section is easy. Looking at the Reach and Page Likes can tell you about the growth of the page. The page summary also allows you to export the page metrics as an excel spreadsheet or CSV file.

Most Recent Posts

In this section, you can view relevant information on your five most recent posts. These include the post type, engagement, post caption, reach, targeting, date and time of publishing post. Clicking on the title of a post will give a full breakdown of the performance of a post.

Likes

Knowing the number of likes on a post can get you excited when building your personal brand. The Likes tab takes it a step further. It gives you the opportunity to identify the source of the likes, the growths, and averages. There is a Net Likes section which shows a graph of the likes on your page. It also includes unlike. It will enable you to monitor the 'unlike' trend and 'like' trend to assess the growth of the page. Identifying the source of likes on your page is also another great feature of the Likes tab. It is also a graph that displays the Page likes from Facebook Page suggestions, ads, or direct likes from your page.

Actions on Page

Visiting the Actions on Page section will give you a better understanding of the different actions people take on your page. Clicking on a phone number, website, action button, or "Get Directions" are the actions that Facebook records. In this section, you can view the following:

- People Who Clicked Website

- People Who Clicked Get Directions

- People Who Clicked Phone Number

- People Who Clicked Action Button

- Total Actions on Page

The first four sections are quite similar. Each displays a graph of the number of individuals who performed each action. The Total Actions on Page also displays a graph. In this case, the graph showcases the number of actions that users have performed on your page. The Action Button is a handy button if you have a unique action you want users to take. It can redirect to a sign up on your website or any other action. There are other tabs available on the Insights pages. These include:

- Reach

- Posts

- Page Views

- Videos

- Events

- Messages

- People

Chapter 8:
Creating A Personal Brand on Twitter

Getting Started

Like any social media platform, getting started on twitter involves creating a great profile. There are a few steps to take in building a profile which will have a significant impact on your audience.

Setting Up Your Profile

Use Your Real Name

When creating a Twitter handle, using your real name is essential for your personal brand. Since another user may take this name, you can use something very close to this name. It will be difficult for your audience from other platforms to find you on twitter if you use any different name.

Just seeing your handle on a tweet should immediately trigger the memory of your audience. Users should be able to connect the name to your Instagram or Facebook account without any issue. It is also like how popular companies like Twitter and Netflix use handles like @twitter and @netflix. Changing your username or handle is possible but is not always advisable. In addition to the need for consistency, you may also lose your verification badge if you have one.

Use A Real Photo of Yourself

A personal brand requires you to connect with your users. The connection should be on a human level. For this reason, using a picture of you is necessary. Avoid using photos of you with your pets or a group photo. A professional headshot is also great for this purpose. You can opt for a session at a photographer to get the right photo to build your personal brand. Being consistent when uploading your profile photo also helps. Having the same photo across your social media accounts also improves the chances of your audience finding you.

Optimize Your Profile For SEO

SEO optimization is an excellent way to make your account more visible. Including keywords in your bio can help with SEO optimization. These keywords are popular words that a lot of Twitter users search for on the platform. Your bio will also appear in search results when a person inputs your name in an internet search. Therefore, you need to make the most of it. It is also vital you avoid the use of numbers when coming up with a handle or name to avoid looking like a spam account. There are certain descriptions you can add to improve your bio. They include the following:

- The target description – your niche

- An intriguing description – something unique and exciting about you

- A description that makes you human – what you love doing

- Description of your accomplishments

- A professional description

- Link to other social media pages, a blog, or a website

Include A URL

URLs offer an easy way to direct users to another site. Adding a URL to your Twitter profile is an excellent way to generate traffic on your website or blog. In a case where you don't have a website or blog, you can use a URL to redirect users to any other site where you are visible online. It can be Instagram, Facebook, YouTube, etc. Your audience will always want to connect with you outside twitter. URLs offer an easy way to achieve this connection.

What Makes Twitter Valuable for Building A Personal Brand?

There are a lot of benefits to the use of Twitter. It is more than using it to get in contact with your friends and family. Twitter offers users an easy means to make priceless conversations with brands and influencers. Users can also join a conversation on a topic that interests them.

The platform is an excellent choice for publishing, finding, and conversing about news in real time. Also, it also provides the opportunity to share other content. Here are some of the features which make Twitter valuable:

Trends

Following trends is an easy way to keep yourself updated on the latest happenings around the world and in your industry. It also makes it very easy to start conversations with other users and promote you promote your personal brand using hot topics.

Ease of Use

Finding users and influencers within your niche on twitter is very easy. You can tag your favorite influencers in a conversation, mention them in a tweet, or follow them. Getting noticed on twitter is as simple as retweeting posts from other users.

Mobile Friendly

As a social media platform, users always have access to Twitter from their tablets and smartphones. It makes it possible for users to comment, share, and tweet from anywhere and at any time. With a lot of people having access to mobile devices, you can reach more users on the platform.

Specific Audience Targeting

Like other social media platforms like Facebook, Twitter also provides an opportunity for users to target a demographic. You can search for users who are fans of a topic within your niche or users who follow your favorite influencers. Paid and organic messages are also available to reach your target demographic.

STEPS TO TAKE WHEN BUILDING YOUR PERSONAL BRAND ON TWITTER

Building Connections and Influence

When developing a personal brand on social media, you are establishing yourself as an expert in a niche. It means you will be someone that everyone will come to for answers and solutions. These include CEOs, marketers, and other social media users. To achieve your goals, you need to capitalize on Twitter engagements to gain influence and connections. There are various ways to connect with other Twitter users. They include the methods listed below:

Respond to Tweets

Showing love to your followers is a sure way to build their loyalty and trust. As your personal brand grows, it is easy to forget this simple step. Your followers will expect a response from you if they tweet at you. The good idea is to respond to your followers within 24 hours. You can make your task more comfortable by using email notifications and monitoring tools on your account.

Tag, Share and Start Conversations

When building your personal brand on Twitter, you may need to share images, articles, or links which don't belong to you. It is a good idea to tag the author of any article you are posting. It will earn you the respect of both the author and your audience.

Talk! Talk!! Talk!!!

Mentions and replies are the best ways to converse on Twitter. If you are using a mention, you are merely adding the handle of another user to your tweet. It is an option which you use in starting a new conversation. On the other hand, you use replies to continue a conversation which revolves around a tweet from a user.

Use Videos When Possible

Building a personal brand will require you to make smart moves. There is a lot you can share on Twitter using videos. Twitter allows users to upload videos with a maximum duration of 140 seconds. It is easy for most individuals to overlook this simple tool, but there is a lot you can showcase using a video. Making useful videos will improve engagement from your users. The use of videos is more likely to get you retweets and replies than what you get with regular posts.

Use Trends to Your Advantage

One of the best parts of Twitter is the trending section. It shows the topics with the most tweets for each day. Take advantage of this tool. By searching for trending topics, you can pick a topic and relate it to your brand. Create a branding plan which will focus on this topic. New trending topics come up every day, if you don't find any topic that correlates with your brand then wait. There are specific rules you should remember when using trends to your advantage. Here are some of the most important:

- Avoid using too many hashtags

- Do your research on the trending topic

- Make sure you target your market

- Remain neutral on sensitive topics

- Participate in the conversation

Twitter Chats

What better way to connect with other individuals than through chats? Twitter chats help you gain new followers and get informed about the latest updates in your niche. Twitter chats are conversations which usually held on the same day and time. The chats typically focus on a topic or hashtag. It brings people with the same interests together for easy interaction.

The chats usually hold for about an hour during which the host will ask about eight questions which relate to the hashtag or topic in focus. Since it is a community event, members of the community can respond to tweets by using the hashtag which the host selects for the event. By participating in such events, you can interact better using twitter. These chats offer opportunities to collaborate and form relationships with other influencers and brands. In the end, you will gain more followers and establish yourself as an authority.

Use the Follow Button Effectively

An excellent way to remain active on twitter is to follow other users. It also gives you access to new content every day. You can choose to follow up to 5 new users daily. One problem when you follow a lot of users is going through all the new content that appears on your twitter feed. There are two solutions to this problem. The first is to depend on the Twitter algorithm for top contents or create a list.

The Twitter algorithm will decide on what content is best for you to view. The downside to this option is that you will miss some critical content. You may still can catch up on recent posts by scrolling down. Creating a list offers more flexibility. You can create a list that includes the important people on your account. The list should not contain too many users, so it is easy to go through all the tweets. Creating a list for influencers in varying niches is also advisable.

Identifying the right people to follow is also important. You can use the "who to follow" tab to select new followers. This tab suggests new users using your past interactions and recent follows as a basis for the suggestion. You may have the urge to follow a lot of big names on Twitter. The problem with this option is that you may not get their attention. Just consider how many notifications JK Rowling will get daily for a start.

Instead, you should follow other influencers and personal brands with a reasonable number of followers. These influencers are more likely to notice your account. Deciding on the right action to take when a new user follows you is also important. A lot of people recommend that you follow back any new follower. In truth, you must be mindful of who you follow.

As a personal brand, it is best to avoid controversial accounts. A reasonable action is to check the timeline of a new follower over the past few weeks. It will give an idea of the type of content they post. Is it the type of content you want to see? During the process of building your personal brand, having a higher following count than your followers' count is unavoidable. It is one of the easiest ways to drive mutual interaction. A follow is a tool to turn the attention of a user to your account rapidly.

Track Twitter Mentions.

Tracking your mentions on Twitter is an excellent way to improve interaction. It helps in deciding the users you should try to interact with more often. You can take this to the next level by using tracking tools on the internet. These tools include Tweetbeep and Google Alerts. You have the option of inputting a keyword which the tool tracks and alerts you if there is a mention of the keyword. It is effortless to find users who mention you more often with these tools. You can also interact more with these users to solidify your relationship.

Become Better at Tweeting

Building a successful personal brand on Twitter will require you to improve yourself in using twitter. There are a lot of online tools which can be very helpful in improving how you tweet. Finding a tool which makes it easier to find and join conversations is essential. A tool like Mention helps you discover conversations which will be of interest as well as those that involve you. It also allows you to reply with ease directly from the application. Having a scheduling tool is also helpful. You can use this tool in deciding the right time to tweet. Hootsuite and Klout are two useful scheduling tools. They both offer some unique features which attract different users.

Use Pinned Tweets

Twitter allows users to pin a single tweet. The pinned tweet appears at the top of the page. It is possible to change this tweet anytime you desire. There are lots of benefits to using a pinned tweet. It can be a tweet that tells other users why they should follow your page and what to expect, run promotions, and redirect traffic. The tweet also remains at the top for as long as you want. Using a pinned tweet to build your personal brand is very easy. Nonetheless, you should ensure you are pinning the very best. It should be a tweet which will promote retweets and clicks. A link should appear about halfway through if you need to add one.

The rate of retweets for tweets with images is 35% more than those without images. It is according to information from the official Twitter

blog. Since a lot of people prefer manual retweets, leave a few characters for them to do it this way. Selecting a tweet to pin is quite easy. All
you need to do is to click the three tiny dots that appear close to the
'view tweet activity.' Just select the "Pin" option that appears.

Changing the pinned tweet often will make it look fresh. As a result, it
will always remain visible to your viewers. A tweet that makes a follower happy will prompt the user to retweet. Make emotion a weapon in
your pinned tweets.

Improve Your Profile
Although setting up your profile is the first thing you do, you still need
to tweak it later. You will need to make a few adjustments to ensure
that your profile is unique. Trends and the behavior of your audience
will also determine areas where you need improvements. Sometimes,
the way you set up your profile may bring in the wrong crowd. Once you
notice this, make changes before it is too late. Remember to be consistent in the message you upload on your bio.

Remain Active
To be active on twitter, you must tweet regularly. You should try tweeting at least five times a day. It is crucial you tweet about relevant topics.
You can start by reading through conversations before coming up with
your tweet. It also helps in promoting engagement with your followers,
other personal brands, and other users. Posting a unique tweet every
day is essential for your personal brand. Include trending hashtags to

reach more of your audience. You can make up to two tweets about trending topics each day.

Develop a Blog

Using Twitter is an excellent way to reach your audience with content that is short and straight to the point. It is beneficial when developing your brand voice and creating engagement with your audience. None-theless, it can be challenging to establish your expertise on Twitter. That is why a blog is a great option. Using a blog to complement your Twitter account can get you the exposure you need. Your blog is the platform on which you pour out your thoughts. On the other hand, your Twitter account is the platform where you voice out these thoughts.

In most cases, your voice will only show a little of what you are thinking. Sometimes, people want something short. As other times, it is essential they have access to your complete thoughts in order to make sense of the things you say.

Chapter 9:
Creating A Personal Brand on Instagram

Getting Started

If you want to reach a younger audience, Instagram is the right place to start. More than half of the total number of Instagram users fall within the ages of 18 – 29. Since it opens an opportunity to reach a new target audience, it is essential you understand the basics of using Instagram.

Signing Up on Instagram

After installing the Instagram app on your smartphone, you will need to set up an account. You can also choose to register with Facebook if you prefer. Using an email that is the same across your social media accounts is what I recommend. It is essential if you want to receive your social media notifications from all platforms in the same place. The username or personal brand name should also be consistent. It makes it easy for your audience to find you on various platforms.

The Biography

Like how you need to create a bio on Twitter, you also need one on the Instagram account. Following the tips for creating a bio on Twitter will provide the right results on Instagram.

The Profile Picture

Instagram profile pictures sometimes appear very small when users are looking through your account and posts on the news feed. For this reason, you should use a profile picture which offers clarity at a small size. The picture should be a clear picture of you – it's your personal brand. The background of the image should be clean.

Description

By this time, it is possible you have built your personal brand on other social platforms. It doesn't mean you don't need to introduce yourself. You are still looking to attract new members to your audience. The description should include the tagline of your personal brand or the slogan. It should also include an outline of some vital information about who you are.

Add A Link

Like other platforms, Instagram allows users to place a link on their account. It is just a single link. It is the only clickable link that will be available on your account. Any link you are adding should redirect to a relevant page. It can be your website landing page or your product page. Instagram also provides the opportunity for users to update the link and make changes to yield more positive results.

Connect to Other Social Media Accounts

As soon as you set up all the required fields, your final step is to link the Instagram account. It is a link to your accounts on other platforms. Facebook and Twitter are great places to include.

Your Strategy

Building a personal brand on Instagram requires a branding strategy. The strategy should guide you in attracting the right followers to your page. To create a branding strategy, you can consider some of the following aspects:

- Objectives: This is where you outline what you are to achieve with your personal brand. In this case, it is usually many followers.

- Select a niche: Deciding on a niche makes it easy to become an expert that everyone will go-to for solutions. It also becomes easier to provide content that will satisfy the target audience.

- Target audience: Identifying your audience is essential when creating your content plan. It also helps in identifying pages that can help you reach more individuals that will be interested in your page.

- Content planning: Consistency is essential when building a personal brand. Here, you decide on the frequency of posts, the time of each post, and the content of the posts.

- Assessing results: After implementing your strategy, you need to keep track of growth. It includes tracking the number of likes, comments, followers, conversions, and more.

How Instagram Can Be Beneficial To Your Personal Brand

It Is A Platform Built for Smartphones

Users who need to access Instagram need to own a smartphone. With so many individuals who own a smartphone, Instagram provides a wide audience. As more users begin to access the internet using smartphones, they will also be inclined to join Instagram. This increase in users will increase your audience.

It Is Easy to Tailor Content to Meet the Audience

One of the facts about Instagram is that it has a lower percentage of adult users in comparison to a social media platform like Facebook. Due to the smaller population of this audience, it is possible to create content which will appeal to them.

It Improves Visibility

One of the significant problems that most personal brands have with the use of Facebook is the cost of marketing. It means that personal brands with more resources can meet the target audience through paid marketing. On Instagram, if a user follows your account, they will have access to all the contents on your page. There is no way to block your content from their news feed. It means that your brand will be able to gain recognition since your target audience will be able to see everything you post. Although you can grow your brand without having to spend, Instagram also offers a paid advertising option to its users.

It Depends Exclusively on Visual Content

The exclusive contents that users share on Instagram are video and photo posts. It makes it a goldmine for a personal brand. It makes it possible to promote more engagement by the audience. Using photos, you can show your audience your personal brand in action. Behind-the-scene pictures also make it possible for the audience to connect more with your brand. If you have a product or service on offer, you can use photos to display these products in action.

Audience Engagement Is Very High

The stats in Instagram posts are very high. It is possible for users to like more than 4 billion posts in a single day. It is a significant development that your brand can use to its advantage. Considering that most of the users on Facebook now rely on paid adverts to push their posts to the target audience, it means there will be lower engagement rates on the platform. Posts on Instagram have a high chance of being seen by the target audience. It will also make them more likely to post a comment or like the post.

It Is A Great Platform to Develop A Personal Brand

One of the features that make Instagram a great place to build a personal brand is the option of including only a single link. A lot of people may consider it a downside. It is only valid if your main aim was to generate profits. Users who focus on just personal brand building can use this to their advantage. Since your audience understand that you are not trying to redirect them to any other platform, it becomes easier for them to connect with your personal brand. Creating a humanizing personality and providing authentic content promotes trust and solidifies the relationship between your brand and the audience.

Building Your Personal Brand on Instagram

What Makes You Worth Following?

Are you providing value? Are you entertaining? Or do you offer high-quality content? These are essential questions to ask yourself to determine if you are worth following by other users. Unless you offer one of these, no user will waste their time following your page.

Choose Your Style and Theme

Any new visitor to your page will be able to see your Instagram feed. The Instagram feed contains your posts in a grid format. How this feed will appear to a visitor depends on the style you choose to follow. The style of your account is the mood or tone of the page. It can be colorful, minimalist, dark, vintage, or natural. In simpler terms, it determines the colors that make your color palette.

As a brand influencer, you need to choose a color that defines you. Some brands may stick to a single color for all their posts. Others may decide on a color which will appear once in a row. What is important is that you pick 3 to 5 colors which will dominate your Instagram feed. Experimentation can help in identifying these colors. The background colors are also essential.

Having a single filter which you use frequently can also help in shaping the style of your page. The theme of your posts is the mainstay of your account. When building a personal brand, you must create cohesion between your posts. There should be a few similar topics about which you post.

If you decide that you will build your brand around fitness, then you shouldn't be making posts relating to gaming. Instead, you can make posts that relate to proper exercise techniques. You can also make posts about healthy eating habits. Your posts should be self-explanatory and appealing to make your prospective followers love it at first glance. For this reason, limiting your posts to about three topics is important.

Your Instagram feed is the first thing any potential follower will see about your page. Having a style and a theme will make this feed more attractive.

What Hashtags to Use
If you learn how to use Hashtags effectively, you can build up a large following in a short time. Hashtags serve as one of the most efficient ways to push your content to a lot of people Instagram users.

As useful as this tool is, it is crucial you don't overuse it. Using more than 10 Hashtags on a single picture is overkill. You can limit the number of hashtags to a maximum of 6 per post. Choosing your hashtags wisely is important. You can start by scrolling through the pages of influencer accounts within your niche. It will give you an idea of trending hashtags to use.

If you are building your personal brand in the gaming industry, there are certain popular trends at each period. Trends in the gaming industry can revolve around a new game release or gaming competitions like ESports. There are two options when it comes to selecting a hashtag. These include the following:

Creating your hashtag is another beneficial option. In this case, you can combine words to have more impact. It is also an opportunity for your audience to make use of your hashtag to get a feature on your page. Here are a few areas that can help in deciding the right words:

- Category – this can be either your niche or industry

- Brands – improve your chances of getting a feature by including names of some famous brands within your niche

- Descriptive – what is the story behind the photo?

- Location – your current position

Using two words in creating a hashtag enhances the impact. Learn to include words which your audience use in describing your brand.

Instagram Stories

Instagram Stories offers users a lot of features which promote engagement between you and your followers. Below are some of the tools which are available.

Questions

It is a feature which allows your followers to ask you questions on your Instagram Stories. You can also choose to give a public reply to each question in another story.

Polls

This feature is like the Questions feature. In this case, you are asking your users a question so you can get honest feedback. It is also a positive way to empower your audience.

Instagram Stories Takeovers

If you want to attract new followers to your Instagram page, then Instagram Takeovers is a feature you must be willing to use. By networking with influencers or brands within your niche on Instagram, you can let an influencer or brand take over your account for a day. If you are lucky to take over the account of an influencer with a large following, then you can gain new followers by sharing high-quality content on their page.

Swipe Up Links

It is a feature which allows Instagram users to attach links to a video or picture before sharing it on their Instagram stories. A significant benefit of this feature is the opportunity to move your followers from Instagram to any platform of your choice. The user only needs to swipe up on the picture or video. There are other features which promote interaction on Instagram Stories. It is essential you prepare to reply to a lot of Direct Messages (DMs) when using Instagram Stories. It is often as a result of the message bars which are included on Instagram stories which don't have links.

Create Connections – And Remove the Chaff

Another easy way to get your profile to your target audience is by following other users. You can also use this method to stay informed. Is there a brand or company you admire? Then follow their page to get information on events, promotions, and company updates. Some businesses also use their social media pages to share interviews which usually don't appear on their webpage. In your bid to create connections, you may end up following the wrong accounts. These are accounts that paint you in a bad light. Quickly unfollow such accounts to prevent any issues. It is easy to become guilty by association when you follow accounts that are quite controversial.

Redirect Followers to Your Blog or Website

Redirecting your followers to your other pages is another critical way to develop your brand. It is possible on Instagram by merely adding a link. The only downside of this feature is that you only have room for a single link on your bio.

Although this is a considerable downside, you must make the most of it. If you run a blog or a website, it is more beneficial to use the link to redirect people to these sites. It increases your chances of getting customers to pay for your services. During the initial stages, you can get more people to click on the link by doing a giveaway or promotion. The link should redirect users to the landing page of the website or blog. Promotions and giveaways may increase traffic, but you shouldn't depend on them for too long. People are more likely to get a full picture of the website if the link redirects to the homepage. Offering high-quality content on the site will make it more attractive to visitors.

Use Geotagging

When building a personal brand on Instagram, you shouldn't underestimate the value of geotagging. The term geotagging implies adding location-specific information like latitude, longitudes, altitudes, etc., to your media. On Instagram, the geotag feature makes it possible to share your content with both your followers and users who don't follow your page. It is also straightforward to use.

If you don't find a geotag that meets your requirements, you can create one through the Facebook "Create a Location" setting. It is accessible through your Facebook account. After submission, you can search for the geotag on Instagram to use it. The "Location" stickers on the

Instagram stories also has the same effect. Since your audience can see your location, it becomes easier to get them to reach out. You can end up having lunch with some of your fans around your location to improve your personal brand.

Improve Photos with Apps

Instagram has become quite popular as a photo and video sharing app. What better way to improve your visibility by uploading high-quality photos? If you can use the various tools like geotags and hashtags without providing great photos, you won't be able to grow as a personal brand. The problem with a lot of Instagram users is that they upload photos with poor quality. Using filters to try and improve the photos only make it worse. Cliché filters are quite standard on Instagram. Instead, why not opt for a photo editing app to improve the quality of your posts?

You Need to Go Personal

There is a critical difference between a personal brand and a business. It lies in how they handle situations. A business is expected to handle situations professionally. As a personal brand – be personal! Sharing a few details about your personal life is okay. A lot of your followers will be happy to see such posts. In most cases, what you post about really doesn't matter – a picture of your cat, you and your partner, a vacation, etc. Your audience wants to know that you are human. Let people see the face behind the brand. Simple steps like this differentiate your personal brand from other regular business pages.

Drop A Reply

There is a reason why this tip is on this list. When building a personal brand, interacting with your audience is very important. In truth, applying this tip may become difficult as your audience expands. Nonetheless, it is an important rule to follow while growing your personal brand. Posting a "thank you" comment can go a long way in developing your brand. The only exception is if it's a troll. For posts which get about 50 comments or less, you should be able to reply to each comment. Although it is quite simple, the primary key to success on Instagram is by interacting with your audience.

Like Photos

Since you are trying to get more people to see your page, then you can attract them by liking their pages. The easiest way to do this is to go to your explore tab and like the posts that appear. If you find a post you don't like, click on the three tiny dots and select the "See fewer posts like this" option.

Depending on how much people you want to attract, you can set your target to 200 posts a day. Repeat this process over a period to get more people to see your page. To improve the efficiency of this process, like posts from your target audience or those within your niche. You can do this by searching for trending hashtags within your niche and liking the posts that appear. Another easy way to select posts to like is to explore your favorite locations and like posts from these places.

Chapter 10:
How to Capitalize on Personal Branding

After building a successful personal brand, the next step is to look for opportunities to make money from the brand. It is common for most personal brands to have a product which they offer to their followers at a price. There are other options available to make money from the personal brand. I will be mentioning some of the options available.

WHAT ACTIVITIES CAN EARN MONEY

Selling Digital Products

Digital products have become very popular with the rise of social media. Some of the unique features of digital products are that unlike the physical products, there is no need for an inventory, and it requires little money capital. The problem of having an excess stock doesn't affect digital products. Creating numerous copies of these digital files is possible. The number of digital products you can sell is also not limited. Online storage systems usually create copies of your digital products automatically to prevent such limitations. Digital products you can sell include mp4 videos, mp3 files, and eBooks.

Creating An eBook

As an expert in a niche, people will look forward to learning from you. What better way to reach out to your audience than through an eBook? These eBooks are informational guides which can be steps or how to guides. Examples include 7 Steps to Becoming A Successful Investor or How to Become A Forex Trader.

Offering Coaching and Consultation Services

Since you have been able to establish yourself as an expert in a specific niche, you can offer coaching and consultation services within this niche. A successful personal brand provides the credibility you need to attract prospects. It is also important you understand the difference between a coaching service and a consultation service.

A coaching service will help in identifying the weaknesses and strengths of a client and offering methods to develop these areas. On the other hand, the consultation service identifies an issue that a business is battling and provides a solution to address this issue. Providing a consultation service to a prospect is an excellent way to identify the challenges they currently face. It also helps in deciding issues which may be difficult to handle. You can then charge for your services appropriately.

Implementing Google AdSense Ads

Google AdSense ads provide an easy way for you to earn passive income. It allows site owners to display targeted ads on their platform.

Getting the ads on your page is also free. All you need to do is apply which will be reviewed. If your application is successful, you will receive an email within a week. There are policies you need to follow to remain a part of the program. If you are consistent in the type of content you post, you should have no problem. There are policies which you must strictly follow to remain part of the program. Part of the policies relates to the type of content on your site.

The ads that appear on your site is chosen on the other end. You don't have the option of selecting the advertisements. It is optimized to suit your audience and the type of content on your site. Although you must avoid coercing visitors to click on the ads, you make money depending on the number of users that click on these ads. Using Google Analytics is also helpful in checking the performance of the ads on your page.

Developing an Online Course

Offering an online course is an easy way to make money from your personal brand. Your audience will have an interest in the things you have to offer. A lot of users prefer to follow steps which are specific while also delivering results within a given timeframe. When creating your course, you can choose to go down the path of an expert or be a curious novice. As an expert, you are sharing the knowledge you already have. As a curious novice, you are teaching your audience a skill as you learn it.

For your first online course, you can choose to start small. Regardless, it is essential you create a course outline to decide how you will transition between topics. Once you have an outline, develop the content. Selecting a topic which you are passionate about is an easy way to boost engagement. The topic for your online course can relate to your talents, life experiences, or skills. The topic you pick should also be like what a lot of people are talking about, but the content should be unique.

Providing a high-quality learning outcome is also essential. None of your followers will be willing to pay for a course without a clear understanding of what they will gain at the end. Your learning outcome will show your followers the skills, knowledge, and changes they will be able to make at the end of the course. The course content should be well progressively structured into themes and modules. You also need to decide what method will be the best for content delivery. Having the right balance of practical, audio, and visual means will have the most impact.

Affiliate Marketing

A successful personal brand is usually one with many followers. Your ability to influence your followers is another sign of success. What better way to use this influence on your advantage than through affiliate marketing? Affiliate marketing is an excellent way to gain additional revenue on your social media platforms. To achieve this goal, you will need to become a part of an affiliate marketing network. There are a few of these networks that rank among the best. These include:

- eBay

- Clickbank

- ShareASale

Your job on this network is simple; you help others promote a service or product. The products you choose to promote should be those that have a very close relation to the niche of your personal brand. It is an excellent step to take to avoid looking like spam.

To be successful in affiliate marketing, you need to be patient. You should also understand that you can only take full advantage of your high-quality content if the affiliate product links you provide are also of high quality. Using a redirect link is also recommended since it appears neater. Since you are on a social platform, why not get social? There are lots of affiliate marketers online and creating a network will be a great benefit. Cooperating with other marketers will offer more benefits than considering them as your competition.

Becoming A Public Speaker

There are lots of benefits you can gain from public speaking. For anyone just building a personal brand, public speaking can help to establish you as an expert in your niche. By becoming an authority within your niche, you can grow your fan base quickly.

Once people consider you as an authority, it becomes easier to make money from public speaking. Everyone wants a moment of your time to pick your brain. In addition to getting paid, you can leverage such public speaking opportunities to gain more followers, advertise your services or products, and increase traffic to your social media pages.

Hosting Webinars

A webinar is an online form of a seminar. In simpler terms, it is a seminar which you conduct over the internet. One of the main benefits of webinars is the reduction in costs since you are not renting a location. Webinars can be very profitable if you use it correctly. To make it work, you need many people who are willing to tune in to the webinar. Therefore, it is excellent for anyone who runs a personal brand.

The content of the webinar or the presentation itself is usually free. It is how you attract more people to the brand. To make money from the webinar, you should offer a paid product at the end of the program. If the information you offer during the webinar is of high quality and there has been adequate promotion to attract people, you can sell a lot of your products. A user will only be willing to pay for your information if they can learn a lot from the free webinar. You should consider the webinar as a free trial of your product.

It is also important you understand human nature when hosting a webinar. It is common to notice a drop in your attendees after about 45 minutes into the webinar. It is why it is crucial that you pitch the product after about 30 minutes into the webinar. Infographics and visuals also aid your pitch to a high degree.

Capitalizing on Crowdfunding

Diving into new projects is an excellent way to make things go better for your brand. Sometimes, the main limitation is the lack of funds. Your brand can help in achieving the funds you require. If you have an exciting idea to share, you can reach out to crowdfunding networks and your audience to raise funds. The funds may be necessary to cover the production costs or purchase equipment of a higher quality.

Providing a sneak preview to your audience is an easy way to get people interested in the project. It means you need to create time to make a great video. The video should explain what the project is about and showcase a little bit of the project. Kickstarter and Indiegogo are popular crowdfunding websites you can visit. These are sites which are very popular among YouTube users. Fan Funding streams is another option which is available to raise donations from your audience. All through the development of your brand, you have depended on your high-quality content. If the audience loves your content, it is easier to get them to support your page.

Selling A License to Your Content

One of the popular methods of gaining recognition on social platforms like YouTube is by sharing a video that goes viral. For any video to go viral, there must be a reasonable amount of appeal. It is what you leverage for an additional income.

Since the viral video is your creation, you own the rights to the use of the videos. Various content creators from online news websites, TV news outlets, Morning shows, and more can reach out. Everyone will be rushing to gain the rights to this video. There are also other online marketplaces which make it easy for both you as the creator and any potential buyer. By listing the content on the marketplace, it is easier for the buyer to find the content they need. An example of such a marketplace is Junken Media.

Becoming A Member of the YouTube Partner Program
As a personal brand, building a YouTube channel with a large following will provide opportunities to make money. The YouTube Partner Program is the chance to make money through adverts. This program is usually more beneficial to channels that already generate a lot of views and clicks. As a successful personal brand channel, it means you can profit from this program. There are a few steps you need to take to become a part of the program. I will be discussing these steps below.

Signing Up
The first step is to sign up for the YouTube Partner Program. Channels that have generated a minimum of 10,000-lifetime views of YouTube are eligible to join the program. There is also an age restriction on the use of the YouTube payment system. The payment system is only available

to individuals who are 18 or older. In a case where you are below this age, ask someone who meets the age requirements to open a family account. The Program is available in only some countries, so you need to check if you live in a country on the list.

Activate Monetization and Accept the Terms of The Program

On your YouTube account, go to the channels tab and open the Status features. Locate the "Monetization" tab and select the "Enable" option. You will also need to read the terms of the YouTube Partner Program. It is important you understand these terms before you agree and click on the "accept" option. Some of the terms include providing original content on your page. It is also essential you go over the YouTube community guidelines to ensure you are in good standing.

Choose Your Monetizing Options and Approve Your Enrolment

There are three options available when monetizing. These include Videos Contain a Product Placement, Overlay In-Video Ads, and TrueView In-Stream Ads. The Videos Contain a Product Placement implies that an ad or short commercial will play before your video starts playing. It is also the same in the TrueView In-Stream Ads.

The Overlay In-Video Ads will add a banner which will take space on the video window while it plays. The ads will appear automatically on your page regardless of the option. You can choose one option or decide to select the three options. The opportunity to adjust the types of ads will be available in the future. The next step is to select the "Monetize My Videos" to approve your enrolment into the YouTube Partner Program.

Wait for A Reply

If you follow the YouTube community guidelines, you should receive approval. It is usually within a short time. Once your application is confirmed, there will be a "Partner Verified" status on your YouTube channel. The adverts you select during your sign-up process will immediately start to appear on the channel. It implies that you immediately begin earning from the program.

It is also possible to not receive approval. It means that the content on your channel has been assessed doesn't appear to be authentic. Violence, sexually explicit content, and hate speech in your videos may also affect your chances. You can choose to remove these videos and then apply for the program later.

Chapter 11:
Strategies for Success in Personal Branding

Having Good Role Models

Selecting a role model often has a way of shaping the life of an individual. A good role model is a person who has a decent character with the right morals. A role model should also be at the top in their field.

Being realistic in your expectations is also important when deciding on a role model. You should expect them to have a few flaws. Nonetheless, these weaknesses should not limit their ability to inspire others. By learning from a role model, it is possible to develop strength from weaknesses. They teach us that your shortcomings should not be a hindrance to our goals.

Getting Motivation from Role Models

When working towards a goal, it is common to start with enthusiasm and high spirits. As humans, difficulties and challenges can quell any excitement you had about a goal. A good role model will serve as a source of motivation in achieving your goals. They will make it possible for you to rise above any challenge or difficulty. It is because they will have a lot of experience since they have faced most of the challenges at different points in their life.

Finding the Right Role Models

Family

In life, the first people we consider to be our role models are our parents and grandparents. Since they are the people, we interact with more during our early years, it is easier to learn their principles and values. The struggles and stories of our parents can serve as a learning opportunity. It is an easy way to identify the path they took that led to failures and those that led to success. The lessons available to serve as a guide is quite extensive.

Learning from History

Historical records are an excellent place to find individuals that can serve as excellent role models. It is also possible to find individuals from different areas of life. It doesn't matter if your interest is in science, showbiz, personal brand, politics, and others. So many vital people fall into these various categories. Anyone from the list can quickly illuminate your life and direct you to the right path.

Biographies

People who make an impact are always the center of focus. Therefore, there are usually biographies about them. Going through the biography of an individual will give you a clear picture of the steps they took to become successful. Some high achievers required a lot of hard work and determination to reach success. Others may have been lucky along the way. The biography of an individual will show the important aspects you can add to your routine.

Have Multiple Role Models

Having multiple role models can help in developing your life at its various stages. Multiple role models also offer a lot of good qualities which you can identify and combine to improve your life. Remember, one role model cannot have all the qualities that will be beneficial to you.

Select the Right Mentors

A lot of times, personal brand owners do not look for the right mentor early enough. They Give reason like, 'why would I need a mentor?' 'Who is capable of mentoring me?' There is nothing bad in paying for mentors. It can be through private arrange a coach or a personal brand mentor. You should be aware that most states have a mentoring program that is run by the government. These programs are often subsidized to give the small-scale personal brand the opportunity to partake. I will provide them with the privilege to access the expertise and advice from personal brand owners that are more experienced.

If you don't have the means to pay for mentoring, you can arrange for an unpaid mentor who would be pleased to spend some time with you every few months. You should not take much of their time since they are offering you free service. Therefore, make sure you give the relationship the respect it deserves, keep the duration of your meeting with them as short as possible, and appreciate them warmly at the end of each session.

Anybody that volunteers to mentor you without collecting a dime is helping you in a significant way. So, it is important to consider anything you can do to reciprocate the kind gesture. You will be amazed at the generosity of some influential people when you asked them for advice. The problem is the only few people have the nerve to ask questions.

Block Out Negativity

It is not uncommon for your friend, family, and even your schoolmates to have a varying opinion about your new personal brand. They will always have one or two things to say about what you are doing. People that do not own a personal brand often fall into these two categories:

- The ones that give you encouragement to carry on with anything you are doing. Regardless of what you are involved in, they will always cheer you up to continue. Those categories of people are just doing the polite thing. "You are doing great," "oh, what a great idea you have got,"

- The second category of people are the ones that discourage you from taking a risk. These are the kind of people who always think about the negative side of the situation. Such people will always say – "Do you have what it takes to get on twitter- what you do something wrong? That's going to affect your brand negatively",

> "Do you think it is advisable to change the color of your brand to Red? Please don't stop the customers because red means stop."

The Advice here is to block out people that always discourage you from forging ahead with your plans. Do not take the advice of the naysayers and never buy into everything the first category of people is saying either. All you need to do is get yourself a group of personal brand owners that agree with your line of thought and move with people who have the perfect understanding of what you are going through.

It is essential you hang out with people with a good vision for their lives and personal brand. You should think about the attitude of people you are moving it whether it is good for your mindset.

Yes, there is a likelihood of negative publicity. You will attract more negative attention if you misrepresent yourself, get involved in some controversial issue, r you misinterpret someone in an article. You should know the more you put yourself out there, the higher the chances of this happening. It is one of the risks associated with content creation and social media marketing, but the issue with personal marketing is that there is no simple way to reduce it.

Once you are stigmatized or you have a bad reputation, it can be difficult to redeem your image, the stigma could follow you for the rest of your life. A bad reputation can result from a google search bringing up the incident, which could affect the future.

Although there are some potential drawbacks of personal branding, it is still an excellent strategy for personal brand owners and job seekers. It is indispensable in this modern world. You can meticulously work to maximize the benefits if you are aware of the risks involved. You can strategically mitigate the risk while you maximize the gains. Just like any other career venture, it is essential you reexamine your effort along the way, estimating your return on investment. You can always withdraw if it feels like the venture is no longer worth it.

Measuring Analytics Via Social Media

The first thing you need to understand about social media is how it can help you estimate the power and reach of your customer's through social media platforms. That is, these metrics help to gauge the performance of the social media channel. Then, you can make use of the information to analyze your content to optimize a strategy to develop your personal brand. Click-through rate is an excellent example of social media analytic metric. The click-through rate is the percentage of people clicking your link via social media updates to your actual website.

It looks simple enough, but it is not so, it can be quite complicated. This is because analytics involves lots of data. The information is processed and analyzed to develop a social media strategy that is in line with your target. The analysis is based on the combination of expertise and experience in this area. You can get insight into an area like audience growth, content arrangement, and customer service through social media services. Are you willing to attract new customer through your social media? Are you posting something that will engage the customers? How fast does your customer service team attend to customers' need through social media? Are you getting a positive response from your customers? You will get an answer to these questions and many other related questions from social media analytics.

Leveraging the Numbers to Increase Your Market Presence

It may be a bit confusing here; analytics is entirely different from simple engagement through social media. It is straightforward to consider the number of inquiries you received and the way you responded to them all. That is an engagement. When it comes to analytics, you can find out where these inquiries came from, how you can attend to them quickly, their behavior when during social media engagement. It is what you need to tailor your message according to the requirements or needs of your audience.

Single number or analytics will not do the trick. The more the data available, the better when it comes to analytics. This comprises the data from customers as well as competitors. The social media content topics are based on the data available from the two sources. Also, it also determines whether the content will be in video format, text or graphs. The data may be overwhelmingly numerous, but every bit of what is gathered is significant when it comes to the development of effective social media strategy. You may not have a complete picture of what is required when you rely on limited data.

How Does Analytics Help?

As mentioned earlier, social media is a great tool and can have a remarkable impact on your bottom line if done correctly. There are three significant areas where social media can boost your personal brand' growth.

Customer Service

According to research, about 67% of the customers have meet a brand via social media platform and have asked customer service-related questions through this platform. You can expand your reach by sharing the questions and answers via a social media platform.

Build Your Brand

The ability of social media to build your brand cannot be overestimated. Thousands of customers can share imaging promoting your brand through the social media platform. Social media platform is a fantastic place to share positive pictures of your products as well as your brand personality.

Make A Sale

The primary goal of any campaign is to convert prospects into buyers. Social media is very powerful in this regard. It has been discovered from the latest research in from Sprout social media that 49% of customers purchase can be prompted when you answer questions that are related to customers on social media.

Data-Driven Strategy

It is quite easy to know if your investment in content creation was worth it when you leverage the data collated through social media analytics. It is a continuous process that should not stop with the first social media post. It is essential to analyze data continually to ensure that you are benefiting from your investment. You should not forget that the amount of data that is gathered and analyzed is essential as it ensures that your social media tactic is meeting your needs as far as marketing is concerned.

Dealing with Growth

Growth is constant and inevitable. It affects trends, society, priorities, and technology. As a personal brand, you must be ready to deal with this growth when it comes. In your personal brand, the changes are usually positive in the form of growth. Adjusting to these changes will not require a noticeable revamp of your process. All it needs is a little tweak in certain areas which will account for growth in your target audience. In order to remain relevant as a brand, you need to meet the needs of your target audience consistently. It includes both the new members of the audience and those who have been members for a long time. You can start by updating contents or re-imagining some of your old ideas.

What Makes Growth Difficult for A Personal Brand?

There are various reasons why you need to be subtle when making changes to your personal brand strategy. It all has to do with your target audience. As humans, there are some specific reasons why change is difficult. It includes the following:

It Causes Stress on The Brain

Humans depend on habits to live. It is a more efficient and effective method to complete the activities of a day. If a change is to come, what is the indication that it will be a positive change? Will it be an improvement to current habits?

Using an Old Brain Map on A New Idea

A sudden change can be very hard on an individual if they don't get time to adjust for the change properly. It is the same way a great football player will find it difficult to perform at the top level the first time playing in snowy conditions.

The Unfamiliar

Change is something that is unfamiliar to your audience. It is the same way they will move to another brand if you try to feed them content that doesn't align with their interests.

How Will You Adjust Your Brand for Growth?

The growth of your audience to include individuals from different demographics will often result in the need for change. To effectively adapt your content to meet the growing audience there are two steps to take. Understanding the audience better: when creating your content, you need to learn the different approaches through which you can reach different audience groups. To make your content effective, you need to tweak the content to meet each audience group.

Establish objectives: clearly stating the objectives of your content will help you assess its effectiveness. It will involve assessing the feedback, comments, likes, and general reactions. Understanding the performance of each content will make it possible to improve the subsequent contents to meet the demands of the audience.

Why Do Some Personal Brands Fail?

Personal branding is a difficult task which takes time. The process can be prolonged which is why a lot of people lose focus while others may give up. The inability of individuals to handle negative feedback will also affect the personal brand. There are a few areas where personal brands make mistakes. Assessing these areas can help you improve your personal brand. Here are some things that may hurt your personal brand building:

Not Connecting with Other Influencers

When building a personal brand, you are likely going to be in a niche where other individuals are building their brand. These individuals may have been in the process for a longer time.

By listing these brands and monitoring them, you will be able to identify areas where you can get an idea to improve your brand building. Proper research will help in determining the aspects that these other brands have covered. You can also locate other personal brands that will be willing to become partners. Taking the advice of others who have more experience helps to avoid wasting resources.

Offering Low-Quality Content

So, you finally have a large audience that listens to you. Is it the right time to lower the quality of your content? Reading wide and staying updated on the new happenings in your niche is important. Ensure your writing remains of high-quality.

Disregarding Your Followers

As soon as you have enough followers, you need to pay attention to them. You want your audience to listen to you. In the same way, they also want you to listen to them. Listen to feedback from your audience regarding the content you post. Why do they like it? Why do they dislike it? You can also learn more about your personal brand through a quick online search.

Branding Yourself Wrong

Building a personal brand that doesn't attract an audience is possible if you fail to perform proper research. Your personal brand should be authentic. It is easy to develop your brand if you are natural.

Failure to Implement A Plan for The Long Term

Where is your brand heading? This is a question which positions a brand for the long-term. A simple example is if you decide to offer beginner tutorials on how to write codes. As your audience follows you for a long time, they will cover all the beginner tutorials and need to advance. Will you move on to the advanced levels? Creating a plan that includes this long-term strategy will make it possible to follow a logical progression.

Inconsistency

In personal branding, consistency is a crucial factor. Your users can only trust you if you are consistent with your belief. If your belief changes at the slightest indication of trouble, no one will believe the content you deliver. Your followers want content that offers thoughts that follow their interests. It is a fundamental belief which they do not like to change.

Chapter 12:
Become the Next Million Dollar Brand

As I discussed in this book, understanding the meaning of a brand is the first step towards your success in personal branding. It is also important you know how to differentiate your brand from your business. The growth of social media within the last decade has made it a powerful tool in building your personal brand. There are different social media platforms available and learning to use them is quite easy. They offer access to an audience which is normally impossible to reach.

Taking your first steps and learning the strategies you can implement in building a brand is necessary. Gaining a better understanding of these strategies will help you reposition your brand for success. Your target audience is the foundation of a brand. How will you connect to the audience? Do you understand the need for conversion tools? How do you intend to find opportunities to expand your brand audience?

There are four main social media platforms which I have mentioned in this book. What platform are you familiar with? Have you been able to establish any connections with influencers on any of these platforms? Is there something you are doing wrong? Did you incorporate the long-term money-making plan into your personal branding strategy? If not, what was your goal for creating a personal brand? There are certain crucial personal branding tips which this book promotes. They include the following:

Being an Expert

If you are not an expert in any niche, then it will be difficult to create a personal brand. By taking a quick look at some of the best personal brands and influencers, you will notice that they focus on a niche.

If you want to sell fitness products, you should have both the knowledge and the body of a fitness expert. If you're going to build your brand around daredevil stunts, you should be able to perform these stunts. Another way to build a brand is to focus it around a niche where you have worked. If you were an automobile salesman, you could develop a brand around car parts.

Authenticity

Authenticity in personal branding implies that you need to be yourself. What makes you unique as an individual? You may enjoy speaking in rhymes or cross-dressing. These are quirks which you can use to your advantage. To build a successful personal brand, you must accept your quirks. Being authentic is the only way to stand out in any niche you decide to focus on.

Consistency

All successful personal brands are consistent. It doesn't imply being active on social media daily. It has to do with the appearance of your brand and your content. Are you able to produce content that looks the same? Your followers will lose interest if you move from make-up content to automobile content. They are following you because you offer content that interests them.

Value

Offering value means there is something useful which you offer your audience. It is not all about making money to you. It is more of providing something that will develop your audience. If you are building a personal brand around the laptops, you will want to provide instructional videos. These can be how-to videos on cleaning a laptop fan, changing the hard drive, and so on. Since you have been providing free helpful information, your audience is more likely to buy a product you are selling when it is available.

Networking

Meeting new people is an essential aspect of personal brand building. It involves interactions with followers, influencers, and other users. When creating a network, you can expand to other niches. It is an excellent way to develop relationships which may be helpful in the future. You should also attend conferences and events regularly. This is an excellent form of socialization with other users.

Develop Yourself as A Creator

Creating your content is a good way to develop your personal brand. You should also come up with new ideas. This includes a new product, service, video, etc. You must keep producing new content to get noticed.

My Final Words to You

There are many benefits you can gain from building a personal brand. One of the most important benefits is the growth it offers your business. If you have read this book, I believe you have a goal you are striving to achieve. A lot of information is contained within this book to steer you in the right direction when creating your personal brand. The book focuses on social media as your major tool for personal branding. Social media offers a lot of benefits to a personal brand—it is cheaper, offers a larger audience, better targeting options, and many more.

Nonetheless, this tool will go to waste if you are not willing to put in the work. I'm not telling you it will be easy – good things don't come easy. Read this quote from Jeff Bezos.

"A brand for a company is like a reputation for a person. You earn reputation by trying to do hard things well." –Jeff Bezos, Amazon Founder, and CEO

What I want you to know is that you won't be able to promote the unique services you have to offer if you keep procrastinating. Put yourself out there; take a risk. The power to make a difference is in your hands. I urge you to take that step.

Gary Donald

If you find this book helpful in anyway a review to support my endeavors is much appreciated.